'UNSAFE AND UNSATISFACTORY'?

central bl

'UNSAFE AND UNSATISFACTORY'?

THE REPORT OF THE INDEPENDENT INQUIRY INTO THE WORKING PRACTICES OF THE WEST MIDLANDS POLICE SERIOUS CRIME SQUAD

TIM KAYE

Published by the C vil Liberties Trust in association with the University of Birmingham.

The Civil Liberties Trust
21 Tabard Street
London SE1 4LA

BRITISH LIBRARY CATALOGUING IN PUBLICATION DATA
Kaye, Tim *1961-*
    'Unsafe and Unsatisfactory'? The report of the Independent Inquiry into the Working Practices of theWest Midlands Police Serious Crime Squad.
    1. (Metropolitan County) West Midlands. Police. Serious Crime Squad.
    I. Title II. Civil Liberties Trust.

    363.2094249

ISBN 0-900137-35-5

Designed by Gareth McMillan
Typeset and printed by Trojan 071 249 5771

CONTENTS

TABLES

FOREWORD

The independent inquiry which has produced this report began work shortly after the then Chief Constable of the West Midlands Police disbanded the Serious Crime Squad in August 1989. His action followed disquieting reports of irregularities in a number of the Squad's cases.

Since then, public attention has been focused on alleged failures or wrong-doing within the police and the whole system of criminal justice by a series of prominent cases, originating in the West Midlands and elsewhere. A Royal Commission has been set up - the first for many years - with terms of reference which include the management of police investigation.

The resources and information available to our inquiry were substantially less than those open to the Police Complaints Authority, whose own inquiries are continuing. Even so, the Advisory Committee believes that the inquiry team's careful analysis of the facts which it assembled has produced valuable findings and recommendations, which will make a useful contribution to future debate of these most vital subjects.

The rule of law which should guarantee the freedoms of us all depends on the reliability of those who administer it, and of the police in particular. We hope that this report will assist in identifying how it came about that trust in their role, which everyone would like to be able to take for granted, could not be assured in the case of the Serious Crime Squad, and what can now be done locally and nationally to ensure that such losses of public confidence do not happen again.

PAUL PHARAOH
Chair, Advisory Committee
May 1991

PREFACE

Funded by a grant from the Civil Liberties Trust (sister organisation to the National Council for Civil Liberties), this independent inquiry began its research in October 1989. It was conducted by an inquiry team based in the Faculty of Law at the University of Birmingham, which comprised:

> Mr Tim Kaye (Project Director), Lecturer in Law, University of Birmingham;
> Mr Andrew Sanders, Senior Lecturer in Law, University of Birmingham;
> Ms Anji Ganguly, Research Associate, University of Birmingham.

Mr George Jonas, senior partner at solicitors George Jonas & Co., who act in many criminal law matters, was appointed as legal consultant to the inquiry team.

The inquiry was independent of the Home Office, the police, and of complainants and their supporters.

The inquiry team was given the following terms of reference:

> **To examine, having regard both to the interests of the community in bringing serious criminal offenders to justice and to the rights of persons suspected of involvement in crime:**
> **i) the organisation, command structure and membership of the Squad;**
> **ii) the working practices of the Squad and/or its members;**
> **and to report to an Advisory Committee and make recommendations.**

In line with these terms of reference, the inquiry team reported from time to time on the progress of its work to an independent Advisory Committee, whose function was both to oversee the work of the inquiry team and to comment on its draft reports. The Committee met seven times during the course of the research and has approved this report for publication, which was written on behalf of the whole inquiry team by Mr Kaye. The membership of the Advisory Committee was as follows:

> Mr Paul Pharaoh (Chair), Member of the Councils of Birmingham Law Society and the Law Society of England and Wales;
> Ms Francesca Klug, Director, Civil Liberties Trust;
> Mr Ken Lidstone, Senior Lecturer in Law, of Sheffield;
> Mr Philip Richardson, President, Birmingham Law Society;
> Rt Revd Mark Santer, Bishop of Birmingham;
> Ms Clare Short, MP, Birmingham Ladywood;
> Mr Tony Smith, Fellow of Gonville and Caius College, Cambridge and Lecturer in Law, University of Cambridge; formerly Professor of Law, University of Reading;
> Mr Keir Starmer, Barrister, National Council for Civil Liberties.

The inquiry team would like to record its gratitude to the distinguished members of the Advisory Committee for giving freely of their time in order both to oversee the work of the inquiry and also to comment on draft reports prepared by the inquiry team from time to time.

We are, of course, grateful to all those who have given us advice or information during the course of the inquiry. Many wish to remain anonymous. We are, however, happy to record our indebtedness to the following persons for their assistance:

> Tom Davis, Lecturer in the Department of English at the University of Birmingham, who carried out some computer-aided experiments for the inquiry to assess the accuracy of the timings of contemporaneous records of police interviews;
> Ian McBride of Granada Television's *World in Action* for allowing us access to material on the West Midlands Police Serious Crime Squad which his own research team had compiled for a documentary on the Squad;
> Gavin Millar, Barrister at Doughty Street Chambers in London, for his advice and assistance on legal matters;
> Anita Richards, Press Officer for the Birmingham Six Campaign, for her constant and abundant supply of newspaper cuttings;
> Tim Watson, formerly Lecturer in the Department of Psychology, University of Aston, for making available much of the material which he had gathered in the course of his own research into general policing strategy in the West Midlands.

A special mention should also be made of Hazel Bond, who acted as our secretary for much of 1990, and who accomplished the sometimes idiosyncratic tasks which we have set her without a word of complaint; and of Renée Harris, Publications Editor at the Civil Liberties Trust, who edited the entire manuscript.

Introduction

During the latter part of 1988 and throughout 1989 until its eventual disbandment by the Chief Constable, the activities of the West Midlands Police Serious Crime Squad had caused considerable public concern. Indeed, it was repeatedly alleged that some officers in the Squad had consistently flouted the legal framework for police investigations created by the Police and Criminal Evidence Act 1984 (PACE).

The matter was raised in the House of Commons on 25th January 1989 by Clare Short MP, who requested that the Home Office set up an inquiry into the Squad by the Inspectorate of Constabulary. It should, she said, 'make a full investigation and clean up the squad by moving out the men whose names occur time and time again.' She was particularly concerned by the case of Paul Dandy, who:

> was arrested in February 1987 and held as a category A prisoner at Winson Green prison for ten months during which time he attempted to commit suicide. In November 1987, all charges against him were dropped because his solicitor had obtained forensic evidence which showed that his confession - the charge against him was based on his confession - had been forged by the police. (*Hansard*, 25th January 1989, col. 1155.)

Replying on behalf of the government, Mr Douglas Hogg, Under-Secretary of State at the Home Office, said:

> The inspectorate is not the proper method of dealing with problems of that nature... Home Office ministers have no power to intervene. There is a thorough and fair system for dealing with allegations against police officers and it provides for an independent element in the form of the Police Complaints Authority. (*Hansard*, 25th January 1989, col. 1160.)

However, an important feature of Paul Dandy's case had been the continued refusal of the Police Complaints Authority (PCA) to supervise the investigation - carried out internally by the West Midlands Police themselves - into the conduct of the police officers involved. It was five months later - when the investigation had been concluded and the facts of the case had become public knowledge - that the Authority expressed an interest, writing two letters to Paul Dandy at Winson Green prison in April 1988. But Mr Dandy, of course, had been released from prison as soon as the case against him had collapsed in November 1987!

Having eventually reviewed the procedures adopted by the internal inquiry, the PCA concluded that they had been satisfactory and concurred in the recommendation that the appropriate disciplinary action against the officers involved was a reprimand from the Chief Constable. Yet, as Mr Hogg agreed (*Hansard*, 25th January 1989, col. 1159) this penalty was imposed not for fabricating or forging Paul Dandy's alleged confession, but for having disposed of the original record of his police interview.

It then transpired that a number of other Squad cases had collapsed in similarly unhappy circumstances before the charges against Mr Dandy were dropped, but none had received much publicity. Because of doubts concerning the conduct of Squad officers, cases continued to fail after Mr Dandy was freed.

Matters again came to a head on 22nd June 1989. Ronald (Ronnie) Bolden, who had just spent two years on remand at Winson Green prison, was acquitted at Birmingham Crown Court of carrying out two armed robberies in city banks after the jury heard defence allegations that both interview records and forensic evidence had been fabricated. Judge Richard Curtis QC described some of the police evidence as 'unattractive' and 'totally misleading' and even the prosecution seemed to accept that police officers had to some degree 'overstepped the mark'.

By this time press interest had been well and truly aroused. Several newspapers reported allegations of police malpractice. The Police Complaints Authority had agreed to supervise four of the subsequent investigations. Moreover, the fact that at least five other Squad cases had collapsed in court during the previous 18 months also became public knowledge.

Within 24 hours of the Bolden verdict, West Midlands Police spokesman Superintendent Martin Burton (who has since retired) announced that the then Chief Constable, Geoffrey Dear, was 'taking a critical look at [the Squad's] structure, function and supervision'. As Mr Burton informed *The Times* (24th June 1989), 'It was recognised some months ago that a root-and-branch review was necessary to allay doubts.' As a result of this review, five officers were to be transferred to other duties as the size of the Squad was reduced. It was also announced that the rest of the Squad would be merged in the late summer with the Stolen Vehicle Squad and the Drug Squad to form a new Organised Crime Squad: this merger has now taken place.

Moreover, in order to eradicate what Mr Dear described as the Squad's 'cavalier and sloppy' practices, the 'quality of supervision and leadership [would] be greatly enhanced' (*Birmingham Evening Mail*, 19th July 1989). In effect, this meant that the ordinary line-management command structure of the force would be imposed on the Squad (see Table 1), whereas before it had reported directly to the Assistant Chief Constable (Crime).

An editorial in the *Birmingham Post* on 26th June 1989 commented:

> Concern about the activities of the West Midlands Police Serious Crimes Squad has abounded for many months. The dispersal of the team should not be used as a means of avoiding the apportionment of any culpability that might exist.

Clare Short was another who was not satisfied and, in the absence of any official initiative to set up a fully independent inquiry, she decided in July 1989 to approach the Faculty of Law at Birmingham University. The independent inquiry commenced work in October 1989.

On 14th August 1989 the Police Complaints Authority was requested by the then Chief Constable, Geoffrey Dear, to supervise its own investigation into the Squad under section 88 of PACE. Despite this development, it was resolved that this independent inquiry should carry out its terms of reference. This decision was made for a number of reasons.

Most importantly, perhaps, the official investigation is not entirely independent of the body under investigation. The Police Complaints Authority does provide an independent supervisory element, but the day-to-day work of the inquiry is carried out by policemen - albeit officers from a different force - in this case, West Yorkshire. The ability of the PCA effectively to supervise an investigation is therefore dependent on the supply of information

TABLE I: WEST MIDLANDS POLICE COMMAND STRUCTURE AND RESPONSIBILITIES AS AT JULY 1989

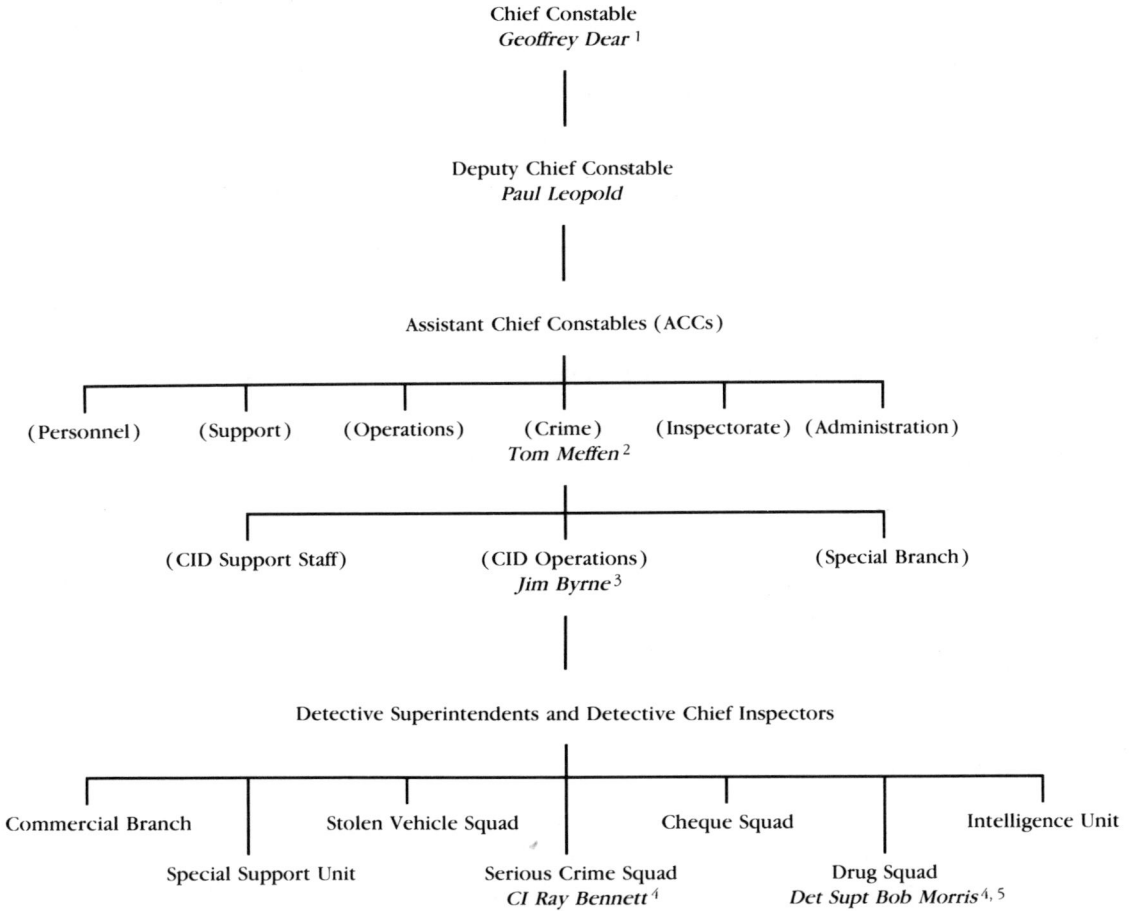

Chief Constable
Geoffrey Dear [1]

|

Deputy Chief Constable
Paul Leopold

|

Assistant Chief Constables (ACCs)

(Personnel)　(Support)　(Operations)　(Crime)　(Inspectorate)　(Administration)
Tom Meffen [2]

(CID Support Staff)　(CID Operations)　(Special Branch)
Jim Byrne [3]

Detective Superintendents and Detective Chief Inspectors

Commercial Branch　Stolen Vehicle Squad　Cheque Squad　Intelligence Unit

Special Support Unit　Serious Crime Squad　Drug Squad
CI Ray Bennett [4]　*Det Supt Bob Morris* [4, 5]

1. Resigned from the force on 31st March 1990 to become an Inspector of Constabulary.
2. Retired from the force on 30th November 1990.
3. Transferred to non-operational duties on 14th August 1989; restriction lifted on 28th June 1990.
4. Transferred to non-operational duties on 1th August 1989; restriction lifted on 30th November 1990.
5. Formerly a Detective Chief Inspector in the Serious Crime Squad.

provided by the police officers working under it. Indeed, we are aware of several pieces of information and documentation in the hands of West Yorkshire police which were not passed on to the PCA until, in an interview on 12th July 1990, we informed the PCA of their existence. Internal investigations of police by police do not generate public confidence, and the fact that so many such investigations have been carried out in the last two years with few tangible results must be a cause for concern. A list of the known investigations for the period 1989-1990 for the whole of the United Kingdom can be found in Appendix A.

It is important not only that justice be done: it must also be seen to be done. The response on 15th August 1989 of the *Birmingham Evening Mail* to the announcement of a PCA-supervised inquiry expressed precisely this sentiment:

> Mr Dear has now called in another police force to investigate the activities of the squad. While it is in the nature of things for policemen to investigate other policemen, there must be a certain amount of disquiet over that decision. There are bound to be doubts, allegations of a cover-up or a whitewash, no matter what assurances to the contrary are given. The police authority should over-ride the Chief Constable and insist on an independent public inquiry.... It would be a traumatic, breast-baring period for the force. But it is necessary. Doubts would be removed, public confidence restored, and at the end the force would be healthier, tougher and untainted.

The problem is exacerbated by PACE, section 98 of which prohibits the PCA from making public a full report of its work. It can instead publish only a brief, sanitised summary stripped of all detail and couched in very general terms. As an editorial in the *Birmingham Post* of 26th June 1989 argued:

> If something has been wrong with professional standards then we should be told. It should not be shrouded by the mysterious workings of the Police Complaints Authority or 'internal discipline'...

Indeed, the Authority itself has strongly criticised the process which, it says, 'gives the appearance of being shrouded in mystery, which detracts from the credibility of the system.' (Annual Report 1989, para. 2.18.)

It is now well known that many people with *prima facie* good cause to complain about police conduct do not consider it worthwhile to do so formally. This is apparent from research carried out for the Home Office (Brown, 1988) and at Oxford University (Maguire and Corbett, 1989). Our own research into the Serious Crime Squad has tended to confirm this. In 1986, for example, the number of official complaints against West Midlands Police fell by ten percent. Yet we have received more complaints about the Squad's activities in that year than in any other.

In the context of this discussion it is worth noting that the Police Federation - the organisation which represents police constables, sergeants and inspectors - has frequently urged the creation of an entirely independent body to investigate complaints against the police.

A second reason for continuing with the independent inquiry was the poor track record of the Police Complaints Authority in relation to earlier allegations about the Serious Crime Squad. The initial refusal to supervise the internal inquiry into the case of Paul Dandy has already been mentioned. The then Chairman of the PCA, Sir Cecil Clothier, admitted that this was 'a feeble conclusion to a scandalous case'. (*Express & Star*, 27th July 1989)

But the result of the PCA's investigation into the case of Clifford Jones was equally disquieting. Mr Jones had been acquitted on 25th June 1989 on the direction of the judge after a forensic expert found that an alleged confession was, in fact, the imaginative creation of investigating officers. Yet despite the inquiries of the PCA, the Crown Prosecution Service failed to bring criminal charges against any of the officers involved, and disciplinary charges were successful against only two of the six officers investigated. (See Chapter Four and Appendix B.)

Indeed, of the 12,500 or so complaints investigated by the Authority in 1988, for example, only about 800 resulted in criminal or disciplinary charges.

In early 1989 West Midlands Chief Constable Geoffrey Dear had asked the PCA whether it believed that the Squad had been systematically flouting the rules. The PCA replied that it had no such evidence. But this statement sits ill with the later, public denunciation of the Squad by Sir Cecil Clothier, who, upon his retirement from the chairmanship of the PCA, commented that the Squad was:

> an aberration. I don't know any other place where anything on this scale has happened. Obviously there is a nucleus of officers there willing to misbehave in order to secure convictions which they probably think are justified. (*The Guardian*, 28th July 1989)

A third reason for continuing with the independent inquiry was the concern that any investigation under the auspices of the PCA would treat each allegation individually to the virtual exclusion of any attempt to discover whether there were any patterns of police malpractice common to a large number of cases. We took this view because the Authority informed us in November 1989 that it expected to be able to inform many complainants that the investigation into their complaints had been concluded well before the inquiry as a whole came to an end. This seemed to us to preclude the possibility that such investigations might need to be reconsidered in the light of evidence subsequently discovered in the course of cases examined during the latter part of the inquiry.

Despite initial reassurances to the contrary, our fear has since been borne out by a statement by the present Chairman of the PCA, Judge Francis Petre. Speaking at a press conference on 2nd May 1990 to launch the PCA's Annual Report, he confirmed that it was the job of the Authority to examine individual cases, rather than take an overview of the police service.

We consider such an approach to be seriously deficient, since many details which are apparently unimportant when viewed in isolation may take on real significance when seen in the context of other cases. Any relevant patterns of behaviour are therefore likely to be overlooked. It is particularly strange that the PCA should approach its task in this fashion when evidence of alleged *patterns* of alleged criminal behaviour is admissible in a criminal trial as 'similar fact' evidence.

Finally, we were concerned that the PCA-supervised inquiry would automatically investigate Serious Crime Squad cases only if they concerned events which took place after 1st January 1986. This problem was ameliorated only slightly when it was announced that specific complaints relating to events between 29th April 1984 and 31st December 1985 would also be investigated. These cut-off dates suggested that the whole PCA/West Yorkshire inquiry was based on the assumption that any problems in the Serious Crime Squad (if they existed) were caused solely by a failure to implement PACE properly. Of course there is nothing wrong in putting forward such a hypothesis in order to test the evidence, but we were concerned that an inability to investigate the Squad's earlier activities and working practices would preclude the consideration of other possible hypotheses.

Our reasoning was obviously shared by the *Birmingham Post*, which was enthusiastic in its support of this independent inquiry. It argued that it was:

> all the more important that West Midlands Police agrees to co-operate in an independent inquiry ... It obviously doesn't have to, but the public will be able to read only one thing into a refusal - that there is something to hide.... The public... want[s]... an assurance from an impartial investigation that if there was something wrong there is full atonement and that any fear of a repeat is removed. (26th June 1989)

We are therefore disappointed that West Midlands police refused to allow us access either to papers relating to cases which occurred before 1986 (and which were therefore outside the scope of the PCA-supervised inquiry unless they were the subject of a complaint referring to an event after 28th April 1984), and also to their own force library. The force did, however, respond positively to our requests for information on other matters and we are grateful for that.

All the information which we have obtained is summarised in this report. The evidence we have obtained shows repeated instances of fabricated confessions and forensic evidence; threatened suspects and witnesses; rewritten or mislaid police records; and delayed access to legal representation.

When the Court of Appeal quashes a conviction on the grounds that the evidence does not justify the verdict, or because there has been an error of law by the judge, the Court declares that the conviction should be set aside because it is 'unsafe and unsatisfactory'. This has proved to be an apt description of a number of the convictions based on evidence compiled by the Serious Crime Squad which have been considered recently by the Court of Appeal. In the light of our investigations, there must be genuine concern that it may also be an apt description of other convictions not yet reviewed by the courts.

I

Methodology

The research undertaken by the inquiry team fell into three phases. The first consisted of basic background research, for which we compiled a dossier of press cuttings and letters from the public to MPs and journalists relating to the Serious Crime Squad. We also compiled - principally from the official Annual Reports of the Chief Constable of West Midlands Police, which are public documents submitted every year to the local police authority - an account of the size, personnel, terms of reference, and position of the Squad in the force command structure from the Squad's inception in 1952 until its abolition in 1989.

It was also our intention to compile a statistical profile of the Squad by recording, for example, the numbers of arrests and crimes detected since its inception. This proved to be more difficult than we had originally anticipated because of the different methods both of compiling and of presenting such data which were adopted from time to time by the City of Birmingham and West Midlands Police Forces. The task was nevertheless accomplished: where doubts remain about the comparability of the data because of such changes in statistical practice, they are noted in the text.

The second phase of the inquiry provided the main substance of our research. It involved the compilation of a dossier of cases handled by the Squad. We wished to include as many Squad cases as possible, but practical problems made it impossible to investigate adequately any cases which occurred before 1979. The reason is that Crown Court archives are obliged to maintain court records for a minimum of just seven years, and most solicitors therefore also prefer to destroy all files relating to criminal law work after such a period has elapsed. Our dossier therefore contains over 60 Squad cases relating to events which took place between 1979 and 1989. We also received information relating to a number of cases concerning the No. 4 Regional Crime Squad, together with some miscellaneous information on other cases.

Although the record of each case in our files differs from one to another in terms of precise detail, we produced a summary for each which concentrates on the following matters:

(a)   the name of the suspect;
(b)   any previous convictions;
(c)   the nature of the crime alleged;
(d)   the time and place of arrest;
(e)   the times and places of interviews;
(e)   the interviewing officers;
(f)   the nature of the link between the crime and the suspect which resulted in a decision to arrest and interview;
(g)   the outcome of the interview;
(h)   the strength of the evidence against the suspect;
(i)   the suspect's previous experience (if any) of arrest and interview by the Serious Crime Squad;
(j)   the nature and subject of any complaints.

Most of the work was carried out by reading files provided by solicitors who have acted for defendants in cases handled by the Serious Crime Squad. It is especially important to emphasise, however, that (unless stated to the contrary) all the findings of this report are based either on documents created by, or on behalf of, the police or prosecuting authorities (but which were supplied to the defence for committal proceedings in the magistrates' court), or else on court transcripts from trials.

These papers have generally included two particularly important types of document. The first comprises the custody records on which, since 1986, the custody officer - usually a uniformed sergeant - is required to record everything that happens to a suspect held in custody in a police station. Most importantly, the custody officer (who must not be an officer involved in the investigation of the suspect's case) is obliged to record on the custody records the duration of each significant event. The beginning and end of each interrogation by detectives must therefore be recorded, for example, along with whether - and at what time - the suspect was allowed access to a solicitor. If such access was denied, the reason must also be entered on the custody record.

The second important group of documents on which many of the findings of this project have been based comprises notes of interviews with suspects allegedly recorded contemporaneously by investigating police officers. It is the alleged inaccuracy of these manuscripts which has been the focus of the overwhelming majority of the complaints we have received.

Other documentation has included written records of evidence drawn up on behalf of the defence and, on occasion, letters written to or by other interested organisations such as JUSTICE (the British section of the International Commission of Jurists) and Granada Television's *World in Action*. Contemporaneous reports in the local and national press of both investigations and trials have often proved invaluable.

The third stage of this inquiry involved following up the preliminary findings of our research by discussing them with other interested parties. These included:

(a)   defence and prosecution solicitors and barristers;
(b)   the Police Complaints Authority;
(c)   probation officers;
(d)   MPs and MEPs;
(e)   West Midlands Police.

The overwhelming emphasis of this inquiry has therefore centred on written material prepared before, during or immediately after any court case. This emphasis has been deliberate. It avoids inaccuracies associated with deficiencies of memory that may have arisen if the inquiry had relied substantially on oral evidence. After all, many of the events detailed within this report happened several years ago.

We have been on our guard for bogus complaints, mindful of the warning in July 1989 from DCI Ray Bennett (then Head of the Serious Crime Squad) and Det. Chief Supt. Jim Byrne (then overall Head of CID Operations), that criminals were trying to 'jump on the bandwagon' of concern about the Squad. As a precaution we decided to ignore any complaint which had not been recorded contemporaneously in writing, on the grounds that it would not be possible to establish whether or not it had been made up in response to the adverse publicity surrounding the Squad. In the event we received no such complaints.

A defendant in a case brought by the No. 4 Regional Crime Squad (RCS) in the early 1980s, Mr Leslie Hillback, claims he was sent three anonymous letters before his trial, one of which was on West Midlands Police notepaper, detailing how the RCS was fabricating evidence against him. The letters also contained allegations that 'things will be arranged so that a judge familiar with the workings' of the RCS would preside at the trial as was 'usual practice'. These allegations were of interest to us. We therefore identified the judges in the cases we have examined, but we found insufficient evidence to proceed with this line of inquiry (which was, in any case, outside our remit).

We have investigated 67 cases in total for this inquiry. They can be broken down in the following manner. We have received well over 100 letters of complaint about the conduct of officers within the West Midlands police. Nearly 90 persons have complained about the handling of 64 Serious Crime Squad cases - involving over 150 suspects and defendants - which took place between 1979 and the disbandment of the Squad in August 1989. (Most of the other complaints received relate to the conduct of West Midlands police officers in the No. 4 Regional Crime Squad.) In addition, we have compiled on our own initiative information about three further Squad cases involving nearly 20 defendants. We have made no distinction, either during the course of our inquiry or in this report, between these cases and those brought to our attention by others.

Throughout, we have been concerned to establish the frequency of any instances of either bad and/or malpractice in these Serious Crime Squad cases. Everyone makes mistakes from time to time, and we have therefore treated as unremarkable any instances of apparent wrongdoing which seem to be entirely isolated incidents (although they may still, of course, be grounds for reviewing the outcome of the particular case in which the fault occurred). But an isolated incident can hardly be considered to be one of the Squad's 'working practices', which our terms of reference instructed us to investigate.

2

The Serious Crime Squad

History and efficiency

The West Midlands Police Serious Crime Squad had humble beginnings. It started life in the City of Birmingham Police as the 'Special Crime Squad', an experimental unit formed in February 1952 to supplement the work of the regular Criminal Investigation Department (CID) in investigating the more serious types of crime.

'Seasoned and experienced' detectives relieved of routine divisional duties were seconded to the Squad and equipped with 'wireless cars'. In 1952 the results obtained more than exceeded expectations. Indeed, the Squad was responsible for breaking up a number of organised gangs of metal thieves who were operating in the city and neighbouring areas in the booming economy of the post-war era. Many of those arrested were sentenced to long terms of imprisonment.

By 1954 the Special Crime Squad was considered to be an integral part of CID, although its name was to be changed three times. In 1955 it was re-christened the 'Crime Squad', when it was decided to establish a Regional Crime Squad - staffed with officers from Staffordshire, Warwickshire, Worcestershire and Birmingham - based on the model of the Crime Squad. The Regional Squad, whose successor is now known as the No. 4 Regional Crime Squad, was based in Birmingham but was given a brief to assist Midlands officers in the investigation of crime outside Birmingham, allegedly committed mainly by criminals from the city.

In 1959 the Crime Squad had its second change of name when it became the 'Birmingham Crime Squad'. By now both Squads had become so highly regarded by senior officers that the City of Birmingham Police Annual Report declared:

> It would be difficult now to envisage the investigation of serious crime in the Midlands without the aid of the Birmingham and Regional Crime Squads.

Indeed, although the Annual Report emphasised that it was not the number of arrests or crimes detected but the seriousness of the crimes involved that was important, the Squad made 579 arrests and detected 1,060 crimes in 1960. In 1986, by contrast, this figure had dropped to just 254 arrests and 660 crimes detected (see Table 2).

Upon reorganisation on 1st April 1974, when the City of Birmingham force become part of the new, enlarged West Midlands organisation, the Squad was given the name it bore until its disbandment on 14th August 1989: the Serious Crime Squad. Interestingly, there is little mention in the West Midlands Police Annual Report for 1974 of the notorious 'Birmingham pub bombings', in the investigation of which the Serious Crime Squad was heavily involved. This omission betrays a marked contrast in style from the Annual Reports of the 1980s, when the Squad was keen to describe what it considered to be its most successful cases in some detail.

The same low-key approach was evident in the 1975 Annual Report. It said simply that the year had been 'devoted in the main to operations in connection with persons involved in terrorist activities'. In fact, most of the Squad's time was taken up in the arrest and interrogation of six Irishmen - now generally known as the 'Birmingham Six' - whom it believed to be guilty of planting the bombs in two public houses in Birmingham city centre which killed 21 people and injured many others. Earlier this year the Six were, of course, cleared by the Court of Appeal of any involvement in the bombings.

This anti-terrorist role continued until the formation of a separate section within the Serious Crime Squad - known as the Anti-Terrorist Squad - in 1979. The main functions of the rest of the Serious Crime Squad were outlined in the Annual Reports of 1976-79 as follows:

(a)   to concentrate on the detection and apprehension of persons involved in the commission of very serious crimes in the force area;

(b)   to provide immediately on request a pool of experienced detective officers to support divisional detectives in major inquiries;

(c)   to undertake enquiries within the force area about very serious crimes committed elsewhere.

In practice, this meant a re-orientation of the Squad towards the solution of armed robberies.

In November 1979 the Serious Crime Squad moved its office from Bournville Lane police station to police headquarters at Lloyd House. This was reported to offer:

> not only... a more central location but greatly improved liaison with other departments and Squads such as the Central Information Unit, the Robbery Squad and the Commercial Branch.

A surveillance unit was also formed 'to assist in the investigation of major crime' (Annual Report 1979).

By this time there was particular concern about a succession of armed robberies, which had become known as the 'Thursday Robberies' because of the day of the week on which they invariably took place. These robberies were carried out by a loose grouping of criminals led by Ronald (Ronnie) Brown and known as the 'Thursday Gang'. In the Annual Report of 1980 it was announced that during the last three months of that year the Serious Crime and Robbery Squads had liaised successfully in their investigation of these crimes:

> Their concerted efforts are proving successful in maintaining the impetus against this class of dangerous criminal.

This is a reference to the now notorious 'Operation Cat', which many Midlands solicitors to whom we have spoken believe gave the green light to some officers in the Serious Crime Squad to indulge in serious malpractice. (See Chapters Four and Five.)

Operation Cat led to the apprehension of many alleged serious criminals, and the 1980 Annual Report commented that joint efforts of all three Squads had:

> met with considerable success whereby [several persons] have been arrested and charged with offences of armed robbery and in one instance the murder of a Security Guard in the course of committing armed robbery.

We believe that this is a reference to John Patrick Irvine, who was arrested with George Keith Twitchell. Both men continue to plead their innocence and their cases are discussed in more detail in Chapter Four.

TABLE 2: NUMBER OF ARRESTS AND CRIMES DETECTED
BY THE SERIOUS CRIME SQUAD 1955-88

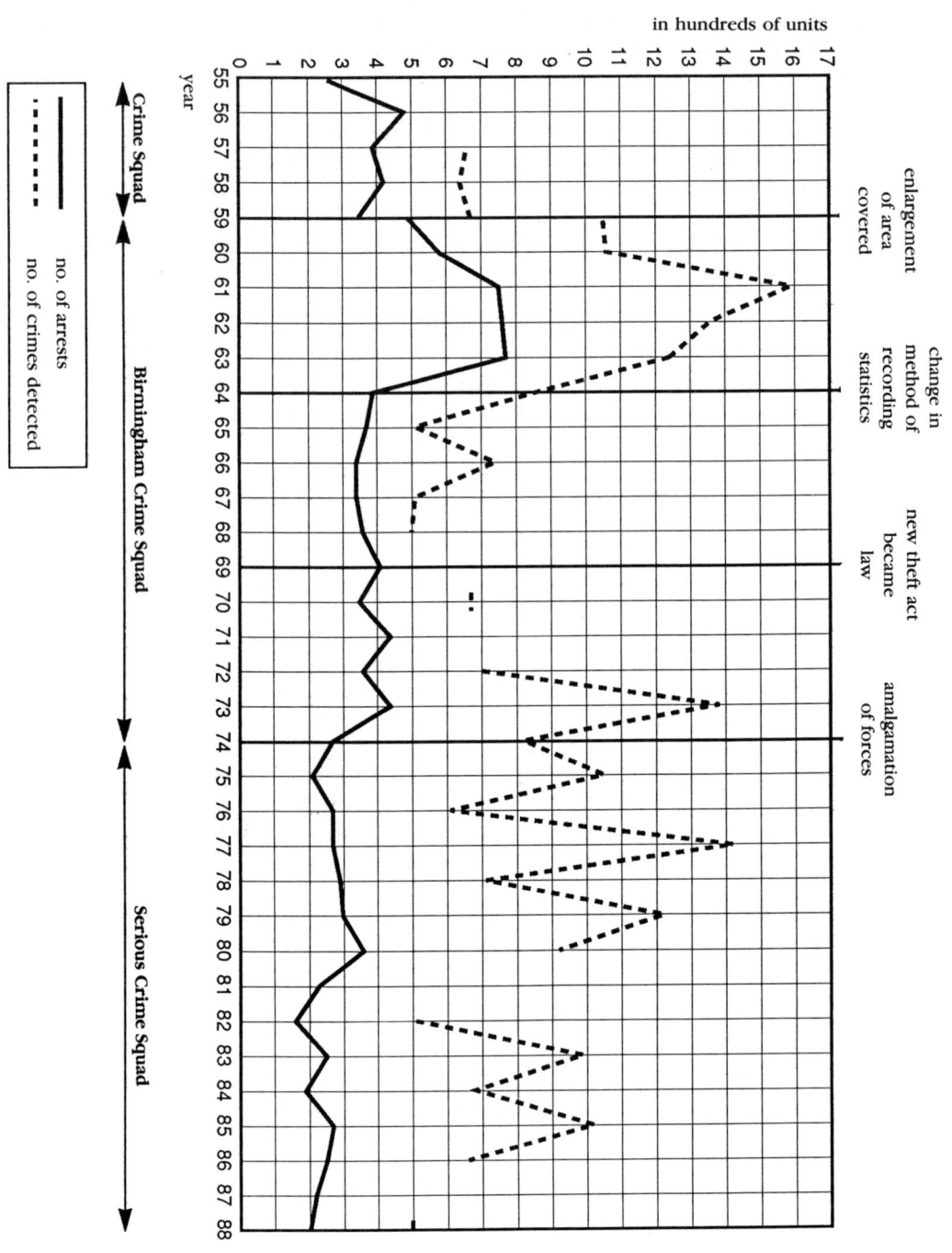

in hundreds of units

enlargement
of area
covered

change in
method of
recording
statistics

new theft act
became
law

amalgamation
of forces

year

Crime Squad

Birmingham Crime Squad

Serious Crime Squad

—————— no. of arrests

--------- no. of crimes detected

At the same time the Annual Report also observed - rather oddly - that:

> There is some indication that professional criminals are becoming very much harder to apprehend, are not amenable to interview at any stage and make every effort to avoid conviction.

But squads dealing with 'professional' criminals would hardly expect them to commit crimes using their own cars or in such a way that they could be identified. Nevertheless, the same explanation was repeated in 1981. No doubt this was also the official justification for the dramatic drop in the number of arrests made by Squad officers to below 200 in 1982 (see Table 2), although the Annual Report sought to stress that it was the 'high quality of arrests' that was significant. Table 3 lists the reasons given by the Squad for effecting arrests between 1982 and 1988.

These figures must be treated with some caution because of the obvious lack of standardisation in the presentation of the statistics . In particular, the lack of a breakdown of reasons for arrest in the 'other' category in 1983 is unfortunate. Nevertheless, analysis of this

TABLE 3: REASONS FOR ARREST BY OFFICERS IN THE SERIOUS CRIME SQUAD 1982-1988

	1982	1983	1984	1985	1986	1987	1988
Murder and associated offences [1]	3	6	9	1	9	6	9
Rape	-	-	-	-	-	3	1
Armed robbery, robbery and associated offences [1]	58	34	38	52	41	50	20
Wounding	-	-	-	-	-	7	13
Aggravated burglary	-	-	6	3	2	-	1
Burglary and associated offences [1]	103	-	130	87	82	54	42
Theft and associated offences [1]	-	-	-	128	120	91	60
Drugs offences	-	-	-	-	-	5	3
Other	-	210[2]	-	-	-	5	30
TOTAL	164	250	183	271	254	221	179

1. Includes attempts and conspiracies to commit substantive crime.
2. The Annual Report does not provide a breakdown figure.

record raises serious doubts about the Squad's effectiveness. Moreover, since the majority of arrests were made for alleged burglaries (only some of which concerned dwellings) or theft, the adjective 'serious' in the Squad's title did not always bear close scrutiny. This point is reinforced by the fact that it is common practice for someone to be arrested on reasonable suspicion of a relatively more serious crime, only to be charged later (if at all) with a lesser offence.

By 1988 the reason given in the Annual Report for the Squad's comparatively poor performance was:

> Investigations are protracted, and masks, disguises, false number plates and other means of evading capture are frequently used.

Such problems have been encountered by British detectives for decades: they can in no way be said to account for the fact that the numbers of both arrests and crimes detected by the Squad had, once again, fallen significantly (see Table 2). And if the number of arrests by the Squad during 1989 up to its disbandment on 14th August - 100 - is annualised, it can

TABLE 4: NUMBER OF CRIMES RECORDED AND DETECTED IN THE WEST MIDLANDS 1974-88

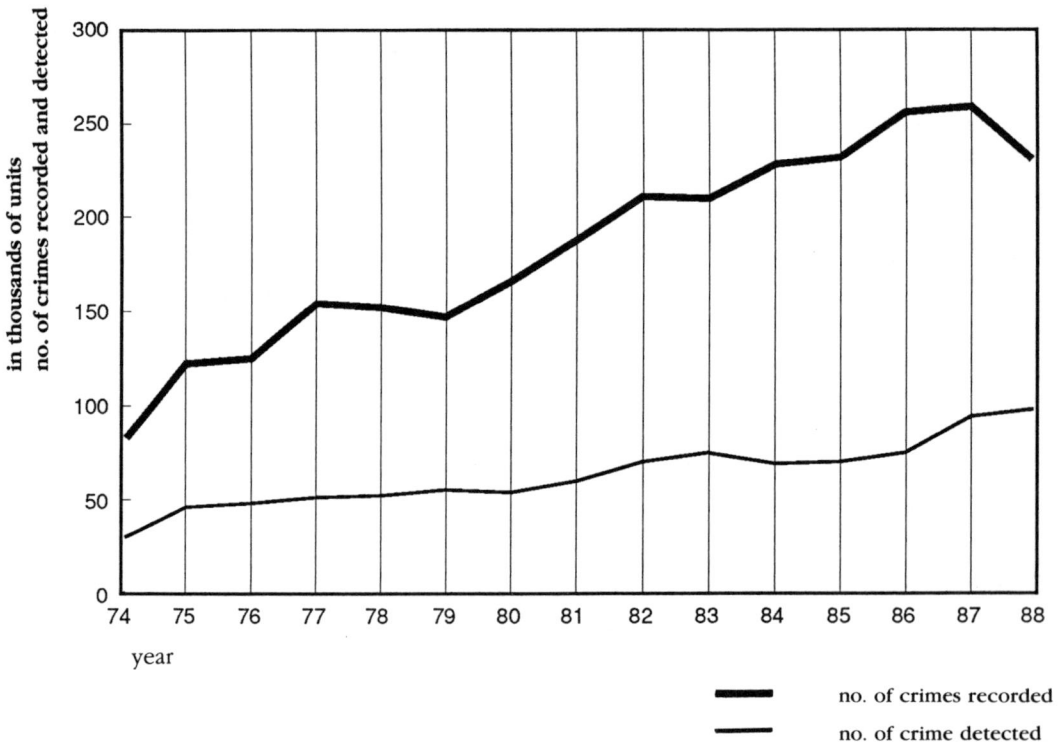

no. of crimes recorded
no. of crime detected

be seen that the Squad was actually heading for an all-time low of 160 arrests for the year.

Table 2 charts the numbers of arrests and crimes cleared up by the Serious Crime Squad and its predecessors since 1952. Compared to the steady increase in the number of crimes detected by the West Midlands Police Force as a whole and recorded in Table 4, the Squad's record is clearly somewhat erratic. Yet in the years following 1982, when there was a marked decrease overall in both the arrest and detection rates, the establishment of the Squad was increased by two detective sergeants and three detective constables. It remained at this level throughout the rest of the Squad's life despite the fluctuating numbers of arrests and crimes detected in this period.

In 1984, when the number of arrests again fell below 200, the Annual Report explained that the Serious Crime Squad had been 'heavily involved in dealing with a protected police informant' - a 'supergrass' in colloquial parlance - whom we now understand to be Mr Albert McCabe. The report went on to suggest that this operation should lead to the solution of numerous offences of robbery, but this assertion proved not to be borne out by subsequent events. For although he had initially implicated a number of alleged criminals, Mr McCabe later wrote to their solicitors telling them that what he had said was untrue, and that he had become an informant only be cause of improper threats and inducements by officers of the Serious Crime Squad. (This episode is dealt with more extensively in Chapter Five.) He was therefore considered to be an unreliable witness and McCabe was not called upon to testify for the prosecution thereafter.

1985 was the year when Geoffrey Dear was appointed Chief Constable of the West Midlands Police Force. Meanwhile the Serious Crime Squad concentrated mainly on the investigation of robberies of cash in transit and of armed robberies at banks and building societies.

The commentary on the Squad in the 1985 Annual Report ran as follows:

> Since its inception in the early 1950s the Serious Crime Squad has been at the forefront in the detection and apprehension of criminals involved in the commission of very serious crime. The Squad is a flexible mobile unit comprising teams of experienced detective officers able to give invaluable and immediate support to their divisional colleagues.

It is clear from our research, however, that by then 'their divisional colleagues' resented their 'support' and were reluctant to call for it. Indeed, the Report of 1986 declared that the majority of the Squad's work did not come from such referrals by divisional detectives, but resulted from initiatives taken by Squad officers themselves.

In 1986 the Squad moved to Bradford Street police station. Most of PACE - which contains the present rules on police conduct of arrests and interrogation - was brought into effect that year, and the Annual Report states:

> a comprehensive and timely training programme ensured that the new legislation was quickly understood, effectively implemented and did not unduly affect police efficiency.

These comments should, perhaps, be contrasted with those of Chief Constable Geoffrey Dear in June 1989 when he accused some officers within the Squad of having adopted a 'cavalier and sloppy approach to the Police and Criminal Evidence Act'. (*Birmingham Evening Mail*, 19th July 1989)

During the period 1974-88, statistics in the Annual Reports reveal that the number of reported robberies and assaults with intent increased by a factor of nearly six from 437 to 2,557. But there was a marked decline in the number of arrests made by the Squad for burglary and robbery (including armed robbery) during the 1980s. This is in stark contrast to the gradual improvement in the same figures recorded by the force as a whole, and resulted in a dramatic fall in the importance of the Squad within the force in terms of its ability to apprehend suspected serious criminals. Table 5 reveals, for example, that whereas in 1980 thirteen percent of arrests for robbery within the West Midlands were effected by the Serious Crime Squad, this figure had dropped to just over two percent by 1988.

Perhaps that was the reason for the announcement in the 1988 Annual Report of:

> Recent re-organisation [which] has necessitated changes in recruitment to the squad. In the forthcoming year a greater devolvement of staff will take place with district branches being established. These re-organisations will improve the already valued service provided by the Serious Crime Squad to territorial divisions.

A better-run organisation would, of course, have realised the problem much earlier and undertaken the appropriate remedial action more expeditiously. But the haphazard and bureaucratic nature of the management of the West Midlands police - strongly criticised by the District Auditor in 1985 and 1989, and discussed at greater length in Chapter Six - apparently made the dissemination of the necessary information to the most senior officers a peculiarly protracted process.

With the benefit of hindsight, however, the conclusion which should have been reached by West Midlands police by at least the mid 1980s is all too obvious. The performance of the Serious Crime Squad had declined significantly. And the problem was exacerbated by the uninformative and misleading reports of the Squad's activities in the Annual Reports. Indeed, the Annual Reports' weak explanations for the low detection rates suggest that the police themselves were acutely aware of the Squad's inefficiency. Such a lack of success would in all likelihood have been a factor in increasing pressure on Squad officers to achieve results and justify the Squad's continued existence.

Practice and personnel

Officers seconded to the new Serious Crime Squad formed after the re-organisation of police forces in April 1974 came predominantly from its forbear, the Birmingham Crime Squad. Detectives serving in 1974 therefore played a major rôle in shaping both the membership and ethos of the Squad. Moreover, as subsequent recruitment continued invariably to be based on the recommendations of serving Squad officers, it is likely that the Squad would have been moulded into their own image. And since the range of detectives with whom Squad officers had regular dealings was relatively small, the pool from which the Squad drew its members was a shallow one. Thus many new recruits to the Squad since 1974 had previously served in the No. 4 Regional Crime Squad, with which many joint operations were organised.

Any problems associated with this insular, isolationist approach could have been ameliorated if the general policy of the West Midlands police force - to ensure a biennial movement of officers in specialist units - had been applied to the Squad. It has been practised in relation to, *inter alia*, the Drug Squad and even the Child Liaison Squad which, since it deals with crimes of the utmost sensitivity, demands a special expertise. It has also been applied to the Commercial Branch - which is charged with investigating the exceedingly complex area of fraud - although many experts have argued that it is in this area that an exception should be made since it often takes at least two years for detectives to acquire the requisite understanding of the commercial world.

Although uniformed drivers usually served for no longer than 12 months, it is interesting to note the exceedingly low turnover of detective sergeants and constables within the Serious Crime Squad. In an interview with us on 9th August 1990, Tom Meffen, then Assistant Chief Constable (who has since retired), insisted that most Squad officers served only for short periods, and that there was a consequently high turnover of membership.

In fact, however, most Squad officers served for a protracted period. DS Michael Hornby served in the Squad from 14th August 1973 right up until it was disbanded exactly 16 years later. His long-time partner, DC Hugh McLelland, had also been a member of the Squad since its reincarnation at the time of force amalgamation in 1974. Mr Meffen maintained that only four officers had served in the Squad for a long time, and that the explanation for the longevity of service of one officer (whom we believe to be Hornby, since he has suffered for over 10 years from a form of diabetes which has recently impaired his eyesight) was 'personal reasons'. But, as Table 6 reveals, there were substantially more than four long-serving officers in the Squad's 15-year history. We have identified over 20 officers who served for more than

TABLE 5: ARREST RATE FOR ROBBERIES BY THE SERIOUS CRIME SQUAD 1982-88

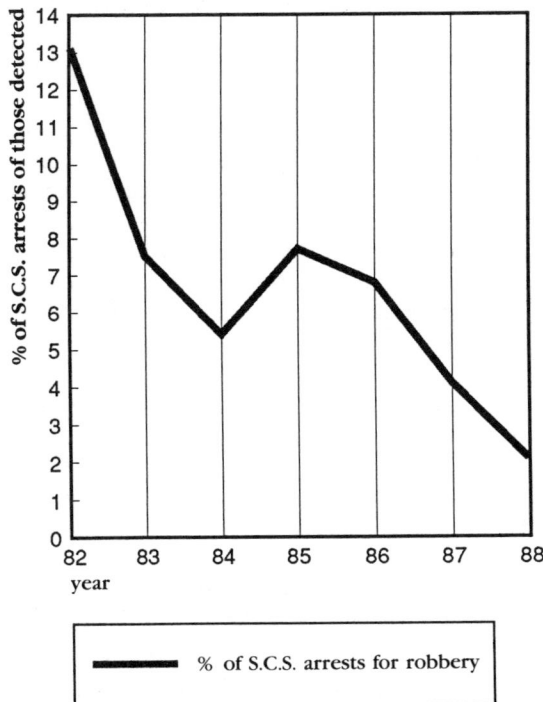

% of S.C.S. arrests for robbery

two years, whilst several appear to have served for more than five years.

The West Midlands police refused our request for an exhaustive schedule of former members of the Serious Crime Squad, and the Secretary of State for the Home Department also declined to confirm to Clare Short MP the years of service of certain named officers (*Hansard*, 16th May 1990, col. 410).

Our own investigations have, nevertheless, revealed a curious paradox. For in some years the number of officers within the Squad - or for a particular rank - exceeds that given as the official establishment figure. In 1986, for example, at least 14 detective sergeants served in the Squad, although the official establishment figure was 10. One reason for this is that some of the officers listed did not serve in the Squad for the whole year. But another explanation is recorded in the District Auditor' s Review of 1989:

> One of the major difficulties in trying to rationalise the deployment of personnel is that a large number of people do not actually work where the establishment says they should be. There is a lack of clarity over who is employed where.

The most startling example given by the District Auditor is that of the Press Office. According to the establishment figure, there were 17 civilians but no police officers employed in the Press Office. In reality, however, the force employed no fewer than eight policemen as press officers, including its principal spokesman, Superintendent Martin Burton.

Squad recruitment policy would, no doubt, have been a major contributory factor to a strong feeling of *camaraderie* within the Squad. However, it would also have exacerbated the inherent tendency of any self-contained group of people to develop an insular attitude and self-perpetuating culture. This, in turn, would have discouraged many other officers from applying to serve within the Squad. The *machismo* culture which predominated was undoubtedly a deterrent to the recruitment of women, and in the same interview with us on 9th August 1990, ACC Meffen could recall only one female officer applying to join the Squad.

The development of a distinct culture was the central problem with which Sir Robert Mark had to deal in his campaign to eradicate corruption in the Metropolitan Police CID. He found that some detectives stayed within the CID for decades, and that promotions tended to be from within, rather than involving a transfer into, or out of, the CID. This had led to the virtual existence of a 'force within a force'.

In such circumstances it is to be expected that the West Midlands Police Serious Crime Squad was highly resistant to any attempt to reorganise the Squad's operational practices. We know of two attempts to effect such changes. The first was in 1988, when the Annual Report announced changes in recruitment to the Squad:

> In the forthcoming year a greater devolvement of staff will take place with district branches being established.

It is, however, unclear as to the seniority of the police officer purporting to instigate such a change.

The second attempt - discussed in the Introduction - was in June 1989 and came as a direct order from Mr Dear himself. He gave it almost immediately after Ronnie Bolden had been cleared of armed robbery at Birmingham Crown Court in a case in which the Recorder, Judge Richard Curtis QC, condemned some of the police (i.e. Squad) evidence as being 'totally misleading'.

TABLE 6: OFFICERS WITH LONG SERVICE IN THE SERIOUS CRIME SQUAD

DS Antony Ball 1974-89.	DC Robert Marson 1982-87.
DS Michael Hornby 1974-89.	DC Alan Pickering 1982-88.
DS James Kelly 1974-77	DS Peter Reynolds 1984-89.
DS Alan Watson 1974-77	DC David Woodley 1984-89.
DC John Brand 1974-81.	DS James McManus 1985-89.
DC Michael French 1974-78.	DC Michael Howkins 1985-89.
DC Hugh McLelland 1974-89.	DC John Joseph Rawlings 1985-89.
DC Thomas Sutcliffe 1974-79.	DS Michael Swinnerton 1986-89.
Det Supt John Moore 1979-82.	DC David Ford 1986-89.
DC Michael Quin 1980-89.	DS Henry Thomas 1986-89.
DC Ronald Evans 1980-85.	DC Colin Abbots 1986-89.
DS Colin James 1982-88.	DC Ronald Adams 1986-89.
DS Danny Lloyd 1982-88.	DC Lawrence Shaw 1986-89.

We know of no evidence to suggest that working practices within the Serious Crime Squad changed significantly as a result of either of these decisions. We believe that they were all but sabotaged. Indeed, Geoffrey Dear himself conceded as much when he said later:

> In June I got the Squad together and lectured them on leadership, on standards and quality of work. Afterwards I considered the matter dealt with and water under the bridge, since to my knowledge there were no further cases emerging. I now know that there were people who apparently decided to stick two fingers up at the boss ... (*Birmingham Post*, 16th August 1989)

Ethos and disbandment

The ethos of some officers in the West Midlands CID is exemplified by the case of PC Adrian Dart, who in November 1983 was the key prosecution witness against three detectives convicted of assault after beating up theft suspect, Mr Junior Williams, in order to obtain a confession. One of those convicted was DS Brian Morton, who had served in the Serious Crime Squad from 1974-76. PC Dart told the court that he had heard a commotion coming from an interview room, and saw Mr Williams sobbing with his face covered in blood after being kicked and punched. Mr Williams later accepted an offer of £5,000 compensation from West Midlands Police. The detectives were sentenced to terms of imprisonment of up to one year and were dismissed from the force.

After the case PC Dart complained of being 'sent to Coventry' by his colleagues. He also alleged that his car was vandalised while parked outside the police station; someone had tried to break into his locker; his police torch and raincoat had gone missing; and officers left the station canteen when he entered. He also claimed that his wife received a number of malicious telephone calls. He resigned from the force after a drawing of him with a noose around his neck appeared on a noticeboard accompanied by the message, 'When all else fails ...'.

The Serious Crime Squad had a particular reputation for vindictiveness. Messrs Patrick Smith and Seymour Williams claim that they were subjected to continual harassment after being acquitted of a post office robbery in 1981. Mr Paul Harris was acquitted of burglary and deception in 1989. After his arrest and detention at Stechford police station on suspicion of these alleged crimes, Mr Harris was, according to his solicitor, 'continually arrested by officers from the Serious Crime Squad for all manner of various outstanding offences and always released.'

Members of the Serious Crime Squad clearly saw themselves as an élite group with their own Squad tie and emblem of a swooping eagle. They had little time for the officers whose stations they frequently 'borrowed' for interviewing suspects. This may well explain the reluctance of divisional detectives to seek the Squad's 'support'.

Officers working in the Serious Crime Squad were organised into teams of three, called a 'crew'. Each crew consisted of a detective sergeant, a detective constable and a uniformed constable who acted as the driver. The latter would seldom take part in either arresting or interviewing suspects, so that operational duties were more commonly undertaken by the two detectives. Occasionally a detective inspector might assist in the arrest of an accused, but this was very infrequent and apparently occurred only when all available manpower was required in order to effect a large number of arrests. An example is Operation Cat in 1980.

But no matter which personnel were involved in operational duties, the prosecution record for cases prepared on the basis of evidence garnered by the Serious Crime Squad in the late 1980s was poor. Appendix B lists 23 cases in the period 1981-90 which we know to have collapsed because of serious irregularities in the nature of the evidence produced by the Squad. Our assessment is that the reasons for the failure of many of these prosecutions are nothing short of alarming.

We have already seen in the previous section how resistant to change the Squad had become. This became even more apparent after it was disbanded on 14th August 1989 and officers were transferred to 'non-operational' duties. (The senior officers so affected are listed in Appendix C.) DS James Bernard McManus - one of the transferred officers - was subsequently seen visiting a remand centre to speak to an informant on an 'intelligence gathering' exercise. Geoffrey Dear was away on holiday at the time, but journalists put this point to his Deputy, Mr Paul Leopold, at a news conference on 18th October 1989. He insisted this was a non-operational duty, but left the news conference without warning when he was pressed as to what exactly the officer had been doing.

Mr Leopold also gave a 'categorical assurance' that since 14th August 1989 none of the transferred officers had been involved in:

> the arrest of persons for crime or the interrogation of persons in respect of offences for which they have or may have to answer before a court. (*Express & Star*, 19th October 1989)

However, the Deputy Chief Constable later issued a strongly-worded memorandum to ex-Squad detectives making it clear that non-operational duties were purely administrative. Detectives could not, for example, visit prisoners 'for any purposes whatsoever' and were entitled neither to wear plain clothes nor claim detectives' allowances. The McManus incident clearly falls outside these instructions. Once again, a Squad officer had 'stuck two fingers up at the boss'.

On 28th June 1990 Mr Dear's successor as Chief Constable, Ronald Hadfield, announced a review of 'the circumstances as they now are in regard to the PCA-supervised investigation into the complaints against members of the Serious Crime Squad'. He explained that this would mean that officers would either be returned to operational policing or else, where the evidence warranted such a course of action, they would be suspended forthwith.

We are concerned that when announcing his review, Mr Hadfield said that not only would he not henceforth inform the press or public at large of the implications for each officer's position, but also that he would not inform members of the West Midlands Police Authority. This would have been disquietingly reminiscent of the findings of the Tribunal of Inquiry into similar allegations of abuse in the Sheffield Crime Squad in 1963, which criticised the then Chief Constable of Sheffield for being both 'barely able to accept that men under his command could be guilty of truly infamous conduct' and also 'over-obsessed with the bogey of publicity' (*The Daily Telegraph*, 7th November 1963). In fact, Mr Hadfield has since announced that other detectives had been returned to operational duties on 30th November 1990, but the status of those officers who are unnamed in either of Hadfield's statements remains unclear (see, for example, Appendix C).

3

The Legal Framework

Police detention

Many complaints about Squad practices concerned the accuracy of confessions and the way in which they were obtained. Police practice in this area is regulated not only by Acts of Parliament but also by Home Office Circulars, Codes of Practice and Police Force Standing Orders, so that it is often difficult to determine precisely either the powers of the police in some circumstances or the consequences of any conduct falling outside those powers. Until 1986 the quasi-legal 'Judges Rules' governed police conduct in relation to suspects held in detention prior to being charged. Created in 1912, these rules were last revised in 1964. The Police and Criminal Evidence Act 1984 (PACE), together with the Codes of Practice made under PACE, replaced them on 1st January 1986. For all but the last three years of its existence, the Squad's operations were therefore governed by the Judges Rules.

Anyone may attend a police station voluntarily to 'assist the police with their enquiries'. The police may compulsorily detain people only if they are first arrested (usually on 'reasonable suspicion' of having committed an arrestable offence). The Judges Rules did not specify a permissible period of detention: suspects had to be charged or released 'as soon as practicable', which in practice seemed to mean between 24 and 48 hours for serious cases.

Under PACE there are now clear time limits: suspects must be charged or released within 24 hours in most cases, but this period is extendable to 36 hours for 'serious arrestable offences' - that is, for virtually all of the Squad's arrests. It is further extendable - to a total of 96 hours maximum - by two separate orders of a magistrates' court. Whilst access to relatives and friends (including the famous telephone call) can be restricted or denied altogether under PACE for up to 36 hours in serious cases, research at Hull University indicates that, in practice, access is routinely delayed for several hours even in relatively minor cases (Bottomley et al, 1990).

Access to legal advice

Suspects were entitled to a lawyer of their choice under the Judges Rules, provided that 'no unreasonable delay or hindrance' would be suffered by the investigation as a result. Research found that around seven percent of suspects requested advice in the late 1970s, and that at least one in five of these requests was refused by the police (Softley, 1980). (It has even been suggested in research by Zander (1972), and by Baldwin and McConville (1979), that nearly four in five were refused).

The Judges Rules also provided that suspects should 'be informed orally of the rights and facilities available to them'. However, suspects were rarely told their rights. Referring in particular to this provision, Sir Henry Fisher's report into the Confait affair (in which three youths were convicted of a murder and arson for which they were eventually exonerated - see Chapter Four) commented that 'some of the Rules and Directions do not seem to be known to police officers'. It is clear that the police often ignored the Judges Rules by not informing suspects of their rights, and by 'bending' them by refusing access when it was requested.

Section 58(1) of PACE now provides that a person held in custody is entitled to consult a solicitor in private at any time. Subsections (6) and (8), however, allow the police to delay access for a maximum of 36 hours when investigating serious arrestable offences, but only if the investigation might be jeopardised (for example, by other suspects' being told of the arrest, or by tampering with evidence). In 1987 the West Midlands Police used these provisions to delay access to a solicitor to a Mr Samuel, who had been arrested for burglary. He allegedly confessed in the absence of his solicitor, and was subsequently convicted. He appealed to the Court of Appeal, which said there was a

> sinister side to... this. The police had, over a period exceeding 24 hours, interviewed this young man four times without obtaining any confession from him in respect of the robbery. Time was running out for them. It was a Thursday evening. Thirty-six hours from the relevant time would expire in the early hours of the morning; then access to a solicitor would have to be permitted ... As he had already been interviewed four times and been in police custody for over 24 hours, the expectation would be that a solicitor might well consider that, at least for the evening, enough was enough and that he ought to advise his client not to answer any further questions... Regrettably we have come to the conclusion that whoever made the decision to refuse [the solicitor] access ... was very probably motivated by a desire to have one last chance of interviewing the appellant in the absence of a solicitor (*R v Samuel* [1988] 2 WLR 920 at p. 932).

The police claimed that they feared that providing access to a solicitor would jeopardise the investigation. However, they did not question the integrity of the particular solicitor to whom they delayed access. The Court of Appeal held that this was not a lawful basis for delaying access. The police had to have reason to doubt the integrity of the particular solicitor requested, which could hardly ever happen when - as in this case - a duty solicitor had been requested, for the identity of the solicitor on duty at any one time would rarely be known to either police or suspect. The Court of Appeal thus held that Mr Samuel had been unlawfully deprived of his right to legal advice: 'one of the most important and fundamental rights of a citizen' ([1988] 2 WLR 920 at p. 934). The decision in *Samuel* has made it very difficult lawfully to delay access to legal advice. Yet, as Chapter Four shows, most suspects arrested by the Serious Crime Squad had their access to such advice delayed.

The PACE Code of Practice relating to the Detention, Treatment and Questioning of Persons by the Police (COP) obliges the police to inform suspects of their rights. This is done on entry to the police station by a custody officer orally and by a written notice. Moreover, section 59 of PACE provides free legal aid for suspects, enabling duty solicitor schemes to be established. Therefore far more suspects are now able to see solicitors than prior to PACE.

Around 25 percent of all suspects now request advice, of whom four out of five secure it. So although more suspects obtain advice as a result of PACE, a similar proportion of requests are denied. Nationwide research carried out in the Faculty of Law at Birmingham University for the Lord Chancellor's Department (Sanders *et al*, 1989) shows that the reasons for these failures - the unwillingness and unavailability of solicitors to attend stations and the actions of the police - have not changed. The research showed that in 10 percent of cases the police fail to inform suspects of their rights in breach of COP, although this was acknowledged in only 2.9 percent of the custody records. Furthermore, 5.9 percent of requests for advice were not recorded on custody records (in breach of section 58(2) of PACE), and the police failed to act on requests to call a solicitor in 10.4 percent of non-cancelled requests (in breach of section 58(4) of PACE). But rather than telling suspects that access is being denied to them, as happened prior to PACE, access is now denied simply by failing to provide it.

It should be stressed that such malpractice occurs in only a minority of cases. However, it occurs when it is important to the police to deny or delay access, and the police are able to complete - and on occasion, to falsify - custody records so that such cases of illegality are difficult to prove (Sanders *et al*, 1989). There is nothing in PACE to ensure that the police comply with the law, apart from limited powers to exclude improperly obtained evidence. There is no more external scrutiny of police practices now than there had been under the Judges Rules, and any reasons which the police used to have for abusing the rights of suspects have not been affected by the new legislation.

Police interrogation

One of the main purposes of pre-charge detention is to allow the police to interrogate suspects. No matter how often suspects may declare their intention not to answer police questions, the police still have the right to put those questions as often as they wish.

Under the Judges Rules a record of interrogation and/or the suspects' statements had to be taken. In other respects the police could act as they wished, and interrogations could take place anywhere as long as police behaviour was not 'oppressive' and anything the suspect did or said was 'voluntary'. However, because there were no controls over, or independent witnesses to, most interrogations, the oppressiveness, voluntariness and even the existence of some interrogations were often in dispute. The result was frequent allegations of 'verballing' - i.e. the attribution to suspects of oral confessions which were later contested.

In an attempt to deal with these problems, COP provides that 'an accurate record must be made of each interview'. In formal interviews this has usually taken the form of contemporaneous notes (made by another officer), but will increasingly be by tape recorder. Also, 'as far as practicable interviews shall take place in interview rooms' in police stations. This means that access to the suspect by officers, length of interrogation and so forth, is all under the control of the custody officer (a sergeant with special training), and all events have to be recorded by him or her on custody records which are available to the defence. Suspects must be given the opportunity to read and verify the notes of interviews immediately afterwards or as soon as practicable thereafter.

Research by Irving and McKenzie (1989) claims that custody officers:

> were not prepared to allow any contact between suspect and investigating officer, save in the formal interrogation situation.

However, either Irving and McKenzie were seriously misled by the police, or the police station on which they based their research was very unusual. For both the Birmingham University and the Hull University research found the opposite to be true. Police officers, as well as suspects and solicitors, talk about 'informal' visits to the cells, for example, yet because custody records are sometimes doctored, these practices can be difficult to detect (Sanders *et al.*, 1989; Bottomley *et al.*, 1990). One officer told Sanders *et al.* (1989) that some officers:

> ... feel guilty about going down there [to the cell]. They're not so sure about whether it's right or wrong. You put it down on the custody record that you're explaining the man's position and then you go down there and treat it as an informal chat.

The casual admission to researchers of breaches of COP suggests that these are routine practices. Consequently, even where the conduct of informal interrogations is within the control of custody officers, such control is frequently not exercised. And interrogations in cars are, of course, entirely uncontrollable.

Evidence of judicial frustration at such police behaviour is to be found in a judgment given by the Lord Chief Justice himself in a case in November 1989. Lord Lane declared:

> This case is the latest of a number of decisions, emphasising the importance of the Police and Criminal Evidence Act 1984. If, which we find it hard to believe, police officers still do not appreciate the importance of that Act and the accompanying Code, then it is time that they did. The Codes of Practice, and in particular the Codes relating to interviews and questioning of suspects, are particularly important. *(R v Canale* (1990) 91 Cr App R 1 at pp 4-5.)

Moreover, the problem will be perpetuated, if not exacerbated, by the introduction of a new Code of Practice on 1st April 1991 to replace that which is already in force. Suspects will continue to have the right of access to legal representation before an interview, but the definition of 'interview' will be restricted so as not to include the questioning of a person whom an officer has no grounds to suspect of an offence, but to whom s/he wishes to speak in order simply to obtain information or to discharge his/her ordinary duties. Clearly, this is likely to bring an increase in the number of informal interviews 'off the record'.

The only way to ensure that what a suspect is alleged to have said under interrogation was what s/he really did say would mean admitting as evidence only those statements which could be independently verified by a solicitor or a tape recording. Suspects could still, however, be 'softened up' by informal questioning prior to formal interrogation.

Moreover, whilst a civil action for wrongful imprisonment is possible where the police exceed their powers of arrest or detention, no court action - civil or criminal - is possible if PACE or COP is infringed in relation to interrogation or access to legal advice. Suspects can make an official complaint. But even if successful, this will not involve the punishment of the police through the criminal law; nor will it provide compensation for the suspect; nor will it directly affect the verdict or sentence in any prosecution of the suspect. Suspects may also ask the judge at the trial to refuse to hear evidence which was obtained unlawfully. But this course of action is of no use to the suspect who is not prosecuted or who pleads guilty.

The absence of any real sanctions for most breaches of PACE and COP thus means that suspects are hardly better protected now than they were under the Judges Rules. In general, therefore, the police have little to lose even if it is proven that they have acted unlawfully.

Police discipline

Police officers do not have the benefit of the same laws concerning employment protection that most civilian employees enjoy. They have neither the right to written reasons for dismissal, nor the right not to be unfairly dismissed, which sections 53 and 54 respectively of the Employment Protection (Consolidation) Act 1978 (EPCA) confer on most other employees of at least two years' standing. In fact, the conditions of employment of someone in the police service are governed by various special regulations.

These regulations specify a number of specific disciplinary offences. Those potentially relevant in the light of the evidence submitted to this inquiry are laid out in Appendix D. Under regulation 23(2)(b) of the Police (Discipline) Regulations 1985 No. 518 (PDR), a serving police officer can be disciplined only if one of these offences can be proven beyond reasonable doubt. In other words, a disciplinary charge against a police officer can at present be sustained only if the degree of proof is equal to that required against someone accused in court of a criminal offence.

In *R v Hampshire County Council ex parte Ellerton* ([1985] 1 All ER 599) the Court of Appeal expressed doubts as to whether this criminal standard of proof beyond reasonable doubt was appropriate for disciplinary hearings against police officers. Indeed, in civilian employment by contrast, an employer:

> does not have to *prove* that an offence took place, or even satisfy himself beyond all reasonable doubt that the employee committed the act in question. The function of the employer is to act reasonably in coming to a decision. (Selwyn, 1988, para. 7.17)

In practice, this means that a civilian employer must simply have reasonable grounds for believing that an employee has committed a disciplinary offence, and must behave reasonably in dismissing the employee on the basis of this belief. The standard of proof required is said to be that of 'the balance of probabilities', which is the degree of proof required in civil actions in court. In civilian employment, the fact that the employee in question is not charged with a criminal offence is irrelevant. Moreover, the case of *Davies v GKN Birwelco (Uskside) Ltd* ([1976] IRLR 82) decided that even where an employee is subsequently acquitted of any criminal charge, the dismissal may well still be fair.

It should also be noted that there is nothing to prevent civilian employers taking what they consider to be the appropriate action before any trial takes place. In the police force, however, a serving officer is almost never dismissed prior to the hearing of a pending criminal prosecution. The effect of this delay in the processing of disciplinary charges against police officers can be startling, since section 11(1) of the Police Act 1976 states:

> Where a member of the police force has been acquitted or convicted of a criminal offence he shall not be charged with any offence against discipline which is in substance the same as the offence of which he has been acquitted or convicted.

No similar protection is available to civilian employees.

Also worthy of note is the fact that regulation 7(a) of PDR expressly preserves a police officer's right to remain silent throughout any disciplinary proceedings against him or her. This right is also analogous to that currently enjoyed by defendants in a criminal court, although it is a matter of debate whether this protection is justified in a disciplinary context since the possible sanctions are very much more limited than than those which could be imposed in a criminal court. (It also ill-behoves police officers to campaign for the abolition of a suspect's right to silence under interrogation whilst they themselves continue to enjoy such protection in a context with far less serious consequences.)

Moreover, this inquiry is aware of no other occupation which affords an employee such protection. A civilian employee who refused to answer his or her employer's questions about any alleged misconduct would almost certainly be dismissed, and an industrial tribunal would be unlikely to judge such a dismissal to be unfair.

A further anomaly is exemplified by the case of *R v Metropolitan Police Commissioner, ex parte Hart-Leverton (Independent, 19th February 1990)*, where the Divisional Court held that documents arising from police disciplinary proceedings were subject to public interest immunity and could not be disclosed to a plaintiff bringing a civil action against the police. Neither could the police themselves introduce the documents into the civil proceedings either directly or indirectly. The police could, however, make use of the same documents in the preparation of their defence by disclosing them to their own legal advisers. This judgment therefore creates a further reason why many people with *prima facie* good reason to make a complaint about police conduct refrain from so doing until any civil action which they might wish to bring against the police has been heard.

Finally, it is possible for police officers to avoid disciplinary action altogether by either resigning from the force or retiring on medical grounds before any charges are heard. Such resignations and retirements have the effect of retaining intact both an unblemished record and the rights to a pension which have already accrued. As the Police Complaints Authority commented in its 1988 Annual Report, this method of pre-empting the disciplinary outcome is clearly unsatisfactory.

The police discipline regulations therefore afford considerably greater employment protection to police officers than that enjoyed by civilian employees. We shall return to this point in Chapter Eight.

4

Confession Evidence

The importance of confessions

Undoubtedly the best evidence which the prosecution can produce during the course of a trial is that gleaned from catching the culprits in the act of committing a criminal offence. By definition, however, the Serious Crime Squad was interested in the activities of 'professional' criminals, whose meticulous preparation for, and clinical execution of, serious crimes would be expected to make their apprehension more difficult.

Information received by the police does sometimes make it possible to intercept criminal behaviour, but it is obviously far more common for suspicion to fall on particular individuals once the crime has actually been committed. Again, the problem facing units like the Serious Crime Squad is that much of the incriminating evidence has by then already been destroyed or disposed of.

Useful evidence obtained at this stage - or subsequently - will therefore tend to fall into one of three categories. The first is forensic evidence. Since most of the cases which we have studied did not involve fingerprint evidence and took place before the availability of the technique commonly known as 'DNA-fingerprinting', it was rarely possible for forensic scientists to be certain of their findings.

The second type of evidence which may be obtained by the police some time after the commission of a serious crime is that from eye-witnesses who claim to be able to identify the persons who actually took part. Most such criminals are likely, however, to wear some sort of disguise.

The third possible type of evidence is a confession by the suspect. Because of the problems associated with obtaining other evidence, it is not surprising that many prosecutions brought on the basis of investigations by the Serious Crime Squad relied heavily on alleged confessions by the suspect. One study carried out for the Royal Commission on Criminal Procedure in the 1970s at Birmingham Crown Court found that in 'a substantial minority' of cases - probably 30 to 40 percent - the prosecution would have been fatally flawed without the confession of the accused (Baldwin & McConville, 1981). It is therefore equally unsurprising - especially in the light of the problems associated with forensic and identification evidence - that much of the Squad's effort in investigating crime was channelled into attempts to obtain such confessions.

The position has been neatly explained by solicitor Torquil Erikson, who wrote recently:

> The work of any investigator ... is made much easier if a suspect can be induced to confess. It saves a lot of legwork. And it can be considered as the most conclusive sort of evidence, if the person with the greatest vested interest in opposing the prosecution actually supports it.

> Every investigator is under pressure to obtain a conviction, especially after a crime that causes public alarm. This pressure is public and external and takes the form of praise and promotion if the investigator is successful; criticism and opprobrium if not. The pressure on the investigator to obtain a true conviction is slighter. For

once a conviction has been obtained, it is generally taken for granted by all and sundry that it was correct. So basically it boils down to the pressure of the investigator's own conscience, or the fear of being found out if he should concoct a confession or otherwise falsify evidence (*New Law Journal*, 22nd June 1990, p. 884).

The potential for false confessions

It is sometimes popularly supposed that nobody would confess to a crime - especially such a serious crime as armed robbery or aggravated burglary - unless he or she was guilty. Indeed, although there is little doubt that most admissions are genuine, some apparent confessions are clearly unreliable. For example, West Yorkshire Police had to investigate a constant stream of bogus claims from men 'confessing' to being the so-called 'Yorkshire Ripper'.

The problem is that there is no reliable method of distinguishing genuine confessions from those that are false. It is, nevertheless, general police practice to rely on confession evidence as the basis of most prosecutions. Judging by the cases which we have examined, however, it seems that the Serious Crime Squad tended to rely on confession evidence almost to the exclusion of any other sort of evidence.

A particularly worrying case of false confessions was one of the prime reasons behind the Royal Commission on Criminal Procedure in 1977, whose report led to the subsequent enactment of the Police and Criminal Evidence Act 1984. The case in question concerned the murder of Mr Maxwell Confait. On 24th April 1972, PC Roy Cumming of the Metropolitan Police stopped a mentally subnormal youth, Colin Lattimore, to question him about a series of small fires for which he believed Mr Lattimore and two friends, Ronald Leighton and Ahmet Salih, to be responsible.

The three were taken to Catford police station accused of arson. But within hours all of them had confessed not only to that charge, but also to Confait's murder, for which they were not completely exonerated until more than eight years later. Not only were they not guilty, but they had neither witnessed the crime nor been involved in any other way. Although there were improprieties in the police conduct of the case, it is important to note that the three 'confessions' were made voluntarily and in front of their parents. They had neither been beaten up, deprived of food, nor subjected to any other form of abuse.

False confessions may therefore be obtained even without the threat or commission of physical violence. As psychologist Dr David Cohen has written:

> In the 1960s research revealed the methodologically troubling fact that subjects in an experiment often, quite unconsciously, provide the result the experimenter is looking for.... Good psychologists are wary when subjects come up with ideal results. In a police station, the ideal result the police usually want is a confession. (*New Scientist*, 27th January 1990)

Psychologists Gudjonsson and MacKeith (1988) have argued that there are three main kinds of false confessions. The first is the voluntary confession, for which absolutely no pressure, physical or psychological, is required. Those who falsely confessed to the 'Yorkshire Ripper' murders, for example, would come into this category.

The second class of false confession is termed by Gudjonsson and MacKeith 'coerced compliance'. By this they mean that after a certain type, period, or combination of stress a suspect will become so distressed that s/he will say almost anything to bring the experience to an end. Far from considering the long-term consequences of confessing, they seek only the short-term goal of getting out of police custody as quickly as possible. Frequently, as we shall see, the police suggest that if the suspect confesses then s/he will be able to leave. The obvious lack of plausibility of such a statement in the cold light of day is not something which a person in great distress is likely to appreciate.

Finally, there are those who confess because the nature of the police interrogation is such that they actually come to believe in their own guilt, even though they are entirely innocent. According to Dr Cohen, the 'very certainty of the police evidence makes the accused doubt the truth of what he or she remembers....[Suspects] become very suggestible'. (*New Scientist*, 27th January 1990)

In Scotland, alleged confessions are inadmissible without corroboration, although in practice judicial interpretations of this provision have watered it down. But it is still possible in England and Wales for the prosecution to secure a conviction on the basis of an uncorroborated confession, despite not only the Confait case but others like it such as that of the Guildford Four, whose convictions for causing the notorious Guildford 'pub bombings' in 1974 were recently quashed. Indeed, evidence which apparently contradicts a statement within an alleged confession may even be discounted by the court. Thus the fact that the three defendants in the Confait case 'confessed' to throwing a set of keys over the fence to the next door house stood up in court even when no keys were ever found; the discrepancy was apparently considered unimportant.

Training in interviewing techniques

The kinds of crimes which the Serious Crime Squad investigated are committed mainly by 'professional' criminals, who are precisely the sort least likely to confess voluntarily. Nor will they normally make a statement which implicates accomplices or provides other significant information. Indeed, they are quite likely either to remain completely silent or else to make up an entirely bogus explanation for their activities at a particular time and location. For these reasons, the former Metropolitan Police Commissioner, Sir David McNee, said in evidence to the Royal Commission on Criminal Procedure:

> Many police officers have, early in their careers, learned to use methods bordering on trickery or stealth in their investigations.

On the other hand, it has been known at least since the Confait case (discussed above) that it is quite possible for people to confess to crimes which they did not commit. It is therefore incumbent on those whose job it is to interrogate suspects to develop and employ interviewing techniques which might assist them in distinguishing truth from falsehood. An assessment of non-verbal as well as oral responses to questions is clearly of fundamental importance. It is crucial that the methods employed by detectives should not simply have the effect of eliciting from the suspect the answer which the police want to hear.

In order to meet this challenge the West Midlands Police set up an Interview Development Unit in November 1986 to cater for the training of officers in precisely these techniques. It was judged so successful that a second Unit was established in 1988. In fact, British police forces were much slower than their American counterparts to formalise training in this way, but much that is contained within the West Midlands training course manual is simply a written record of techniques practised by experienced detectives for many years.

Research commissioned by the Royal Commission on Criminal Procedure (Irving, 1980) demonstrated that such general interrogation techniques had developed a considerable degree of sophistication, in that even in a 'normal' interview a suspect could be put under such psychological and social pressure that few could withstand it and avoid confessing - apparently voluntarily - whether truly guilty or not. Irving concluded that there was no way of distinguishing, merely from the interrogation and confession, between true and false confessions.

The problem is that being interviewed by a policeman, whether in a cell or elsewhere, is a very stressful experience. Whilst it is this stress factor which the police rely on to gain confessions from suspects, it inevitably undermines the apparently voluntary nature of any statement by the interviewee. As Irving himself explained: 'It is impossible to fix levels of stress that would be "reasonable" - it varies so much from person to person' (The Sunday Times, 10th August 1980). It is therefore extremely difficult to determine whether the police may have exerted undue pressure.

Moreover, it 'is extremely difficult to determine what it is in each interrogation that will finally make a person confess' (The Sunday Times, 10th August 1980). It is therefore equally difficult to tell whether the particular stress involved has elicited a true or false response. Not only does everyone react differently to each level of stress: it is also the case that different people perceive different things to be stressful.

In this context much of what is contained within the Interview Development Unit's course manual appears dangerously simplistic. A rumbling stomach, for example, is given as a possible indicator of guilt, although it may also suggest that the interviewee is simply hungry. A composed suspect is depicted as innocent, whilst one who accepts the necessity of the interview because the police are just doing their job is seen as guilty. Similarly, the trainee interviewer is informed that innocent people will 'rarely ... back down from you, they may even insult you'. But a guilty suspect 'feels the more he complains the more likely you are to leave him alone.' There seems to us to be little difference between these allegedly distinctive responses. Moreover, nervousness, anger and fear are all categorised initially as emotions common to both the guilty and innocent, but the manual then deems those who evince 'unjust anger' or who appear 'out of control, nervous' to be guilty.

As a leader article in The Guardian of 19th June 1990 put it:

> [T]he West Midlands training course suggests a dangerously prescriptive approach to highly complicated indicators. It is certainly true, as the handbook suggests, that liars 'may' slouch or adopt a rigid posture. But then they may not: 'may' must not be turned into a predictive indicator. Certainly body language is important; and different approaches are needed towards different suspects. But the strategies outlined look too simplistic in terms of the range of personality types and the problems of conscious and unconscious motivation. Detecting deception is a highly complex issue which cannot be achieved via simple psychological precepts. Rather than give their trainees a cookbook course on modern psychology, the police would do better to adopt the approach of the Mersey scheme, with its emphasis on teaching the police to listen and frame questions. Research shows the biggest mistake in interrogation is the failure to listen to what is said...

The alternative school of police interviewing training mentioned in this article is that promoted by the Merseyside Police Training School, which favours what some psychologists believe to be a more ethical approach. The head of its Interview Development Section, Detective Inspector Frank Kite, believes 'that you can stress people into saying anything' (quoted by Cohen, *New Scientist*, 27th January 1990) but that this can be very counter-productive.

Dick Hobbs, a lecturer in criminology at the Polytechnic of Central London who has studied interviewing techniques, is also sceptical as to the usefulness of the West Midlands Interview Development Unit's course manual:

> By noting the entire range of human emotions as a possible indication of guilt, the police are allowing officers' pre-conceived notions of an individual's guilt to appear justified. It highlights the need for them - and the public - to be wary of psychological profiles. They are not useful indicators, especially in a situation where all participants - detectives included - are in a very stressful situation. (*The Daily Telegraph*, 7th June 1990)

Interviewing personnel

It has already been noted that officers within the Serious Crime Squad were officially organised into teams of three, called a 'crew'. But since one of these officers would be a uniformed constable acting as a driver, most operational work tended to be done in pairs, typically one detective sergeant and one detective constable. It has also been explained that the focus of most of the Squad's work was on interviewing suspects. Since every detective on the Squad is likely to have undergone similar training in interviewing techniques, it would not be particularly important to have the same pairs of interviewers invariably working together. Moreover, sick leave and holidays - together with different shift patterns and rates of overtime - would hamper the Squad's ability to maintain the same interviewing partnerships. The mountain of paperwork required of every officer in the West Midlands force (dealt with in greater detail in Chapter Six) would inevitably mean that officers would sometimes be simply unavailable for ordinary operational duties.

It is to be expected, therefore, that the evidence gathered by this independent inquiry shows that there was some flexibility in the arrangements for teams of interviewers. Crewing arrangements meant, however, that a Squad detective could expect to conduct most of his interrogations with his regular partner. The inquiry team has identified nine partnerships - all consisting of one detective sergeant with one detective constable - which operated in the 1980s for an average period of about four years.

One feature of these pairings is that they constitute a majority of the officers employed in the Squad in the 1980s. Another is their over-representation in the number of cases brought by the Squad where defendants have been acquitted because of defects in the prosecution evidence (see Appendix B). The pairings of DS James Bernard McManus and DC Ronald Tony Adams, and DS Michael Hornby and DC Hugh McLelland, for example, were involved in the well-publicised case of Ronnie Bolden, who was acquitted on 22nd June 1989 amid allegations that the police had fabricated both incriminating statements and the allegedly corroborative forensic evidence. DS McManus also claimed in evidence that Mr Bolden's solicitors had attempted to bribe a witness, Mr Paul Fitzsimmons. This claim was found to have no foundation in truth.

DS McManus and DC Adams had also been the main police witnesses in Fitzsimmons's own trial in October 1988. Fitzsimmons had been acquitted on the direction of the judge, Malcolm Potter, who felt after a discussion with counsel in chambers that DS McManus had been discredited as a reliable witness and announced that he would be writing to the then Chief Constable, Geoffrey Dear, to ask him to clear up questions about DS McManus's credibility. Moreover, a confession allegedly given voluntarily to Messrs McManus and Adams by the defendant was found to have been extracted under duress.

Over a year before, the following pairings had all been involved in the unsuccessful prosecution of John Bullivant and others: DS Mc Manus and DC Adams; DS Hornby and DC McLelland; DS Michael Swinnerton and DC John Joseph Rawlings; DS David Ford and DC Michael Quin; DS Peter Melvin Reynolds and DC John Norman Perkins; DS Danny Lloyd and DC Lawrence Shaw. The defendants were again acquitted by the jury after their lawyers had claimed that the police had fabricated confessions and planted evidence. Another similarity between the cases of Fitzsimmons and Bullivant *et al* is that in both cases an important piece of evidence went missing.

It should also be noted that DS McManus was one of the officers who claimed in 1987 to have obtained a confession from Paul Dandy. In fact, an Electrostatic Deposition Analysis (ESDA) test - which involves the analysis of the impressions on sheets of paper underneath those on which a suspect's alleged statement was written - found that the allegedly contemporaneous notes of that interrogation showed that the two pages containing the admissions had been inserted afterwards. The charges against Paul Dandy were withdrawn as a result. McManus's partner on this occasion was DC Shaw. Both were subsequently reprimanded as a result of this case for falsifying notes and losing a page of the interview record; Detective Superintendent John Brown was also disciplined for the latter offence. In the same year Shaw was also discredited as a witness in the unsuccessful prosecution of Leroy Francis and Ramsingh Nowjadicksingh.

DS Hornby was one of the officers involved in the interrogation of the so-called Birmingham Six in 1974. He and his partner DC McLelland were also the officers who interviewed Clifford Jones on 15th July 1986 on suspicion of a robbery which had taken place six months earlier. An ESDA test revealed that two pages of admissions had been inserted into the allegedly contemporaneous notes of the interview. Judge Stuart White commented:

>...let us get down to brass tacks. Here is a case where the prosecution's own forensic evidence has raised, in the mind of the Judge at least, a very substantial doubt as to the genuineness of that vital document such that if there were to be a conviction on that charge against the defendant I would feel more than a little anxious about it.

He therefore directed the jury to return a verdict of not guilty given 'the wholly unsatisfactory state of the evidence' and wrote to the Chief Constable requesting that he hold an inquiry.

The partnership of DS Reynolds and DC Perkins was also involved in investigating this case and, indeed, they were the subject of disciplinary charges concerning their conduct. Reynolds was found guilty of making false and untruthful records, and was demoted to the rank of police constable in uniform. Perkins was found guilty of the same disciplinary offence and was fined 13 days' pay (about £500), which is the maximum fine permissible under police regulations. Moreover, charges brought against two co-defendants were dropped because the prosecution would have been tainted by the collapse of the case against Mr Jones (see Appendix B).

It is noteworthy that, while serving in the No. 4 Regional Crime Squad in the 1970s, DC Perkins claimed to have obtained the confession from Mr Pat Molloy which led to the now-controversial conviction of James Robinson, Vincent and Michael Hickey, and Molloy himself, for the murder of newspaper boy, Carl Bridgewater. Again, Molloy had previously denied any involvement when questioned by other officers. Mr Jim Nichol, the solicitor for the convicted men, is to petition the Home Secretary to refer this case back to the Court of Appeal on the grounds that new expert evidence casts grave doubt on the authenticity of the alleged confession. Mr AQ Morton, a Fellow of the Royal Society of Edinburgh, recently applied new scientific techniques to test the authorship of Molloy's alleged confession. He concluded: 'The confession is not his. It was made up by more than one person.' (*Daily Mirror*, 4th May 1990)

The cases of Jones and Molloy, together with that of Bullivant *et al* (see above, and also Chapter Five) give rise to some concern about the roles that these officers played in the serious Crime Squad. There are also two further Squad cases where broadly similar allegations have been made against Messrs Reynolds and Perkins, but where there is not the same kind of objective evidence to support the allegations of the defendants, who were convicted at trial. One concerns the arrest on 11th July 1984 of Mr Trevor Campbell on suspicion of the murder of Mrs Ethel Cawood. He was initially interviewed by two officers from outside the Squad, who insisted that Campbell had murdered the deceased woman. Campbell denied any involvement and produced an alibi. Interviews a fortnight earlier had proceeded in a similar way, and the pattern was repeated at a second interview with the same detectives a little later on the 11th of July.

According to police records, a third interview began - conducted on this occasion by DS Reynolds and DC Perkins - almost exactly two hours after the second had ended. This is also supposed to have commenced with Campbell's protesting his innocence, but suddenly he is alleged to have started crying and saying to these two strange men whom he had never met before:

> I don't want my mum to know.... It was me, I want to tell someone, I just wished you were my dad.

According to the interviewing officers, Campbell 'then leaned forward and took DC Perkins's hand'. He is then alleged to have given a full confession. Both Campbell and his co-accused, Christine Sawbridge (who was only 16 years old at the time of the killing) were convicted of murder: much of the case against them both was based on Campbell's alleged confession. Campbell was sentenced to life imprisonment; Sawbridge was ordered to be detained at Her Majesty's pleasure.

The same two officers seem to have been able to obtain an equally unexpected confession in similar circumstances in the case of George Glen Lewis, who had been interviewed by divisional detectives on 16th January 1987 in connection with a burglary. Lewis categorically denied any involvement. On 21st January 1987, however, he was arrested by Messrs. Reynolds and Perkins, who took him to Wednesfield Police Station for interrogation. After administering the required caution, it allegedly began:

DS Perkins: Firstly let's talk about the burglary that happened last week at Tettenhall.
Lewis: The police have already interviewed me about it. I did it.

A full confession is then supposed to have been forthcoming.

Paul Harris was arrested on 23rd October 1987 on suspicion of burglary and deception. When initially interviewed, he admitted nothing. But when interrogated by Messrs Hornby and McLelland, they claim that he confessed to certain crimes, although he refused to sign their notes as an accurate record of the proceedings. At the trial on 25th April 1989, the prosecution decided to offer no evidence against Mr Harris and the judge ordered the jury to bring in a verdict of not guilty.

Hassan Khan was arrested on the evening of 20th November 1987 in Caernarvon, North Wales, on suspicion of robbing a Dixons store in Birmingham city centre two months earlier. DS Swinnerton, DC Rawlings and DC Michael Howkins claimed that, during the car journey back to Chelmsley Wood police station in Birmingham and without any prompting from them, Mr Khan confessed to the robbery. The detectives alleged that everything Khan said was written down by DS Swinnerton by the light of a torch hung round his neck as he sat in the front passenger seat.

On the afternoon of 21st November Khan was interviewed again. On this occasion the officers involved were DC Howkins and DS Leary. Again Khan is alleged to have admitted his part in the robbery, although he apparently refused to sign a statement to that effect. This meant, they claimed, that Detective Inspector Robert Goodchild had to read it back to him. Hassan Khan maintained throughout that the officers' accounts of these interrogations were a complete fabrication.

Dr Malcolm Coulthard, a linguistics expert from Birmingham University, cast doubt on the authenticity of the alleged confession in the car. In the Court of Appeal, the Lord Chief Justice, Lord Lane, was more forthright:

> It is a remarkable fact that the notes allegedly written by torchlight in a moving car show no signs of the pen being jolted and no difference from other notes written in the police station. Secondly, in the statement allegedly made on 21 November, there was no reference to any conversation in the car. Thirdly, there seems to be no reason why he should not have signed the statement if he was freely admitting his guilt. Fourthly, the senior officer who endorsed the statement was not an independent uniformed officer but a member of the crime squad.

The Court of Appeal therefore quashed Khan's conviction.

The combination of Messrs Swinnerton and Rawlings also seems to have been remarkably successful in extracting a speedy - albeit disputed - confession. Having been interviewed earlier about a robbery at Gooch Street Post Office, when his answers were apparently evasive, Carlton Colin Alladice is alleged to have confessed after just about a quarter of an hour of being interviewed by DS Swinnerton and DC Rawlings:

> You know what happened at the post office. We went behind the counter and took the money. That's what you want to hear. I've told you my part now.

The lack of detail in this statement is striking. Yet the rest of the interview is claimed to have lasted only about another ten minutes. The inquiry team finds it difficult to believe that trained detectives would not have persisted with such an apparently successful line of questioning for rather longer. Moreover, only two of the subsequent five questions were apparently intended to elucidate further information about the method of robbery. This is not the usual way to gather evidence or to test the truth of a confession. Mr Alladice denies ever having made the confession. Although he was convicted, the inquiry team nevertheless feels that there are legitimate grounds for concern that this interview was allowed into court as part of the evidence against him.

It should be noted, however, that complaints about the fabrication of evidence are by no means restricted to the regular pairings. An example is Detective Inspector Paul Matthews, who was one of the officers who helped to obtain a confession in 1974 from Mr Paddy Hill, one of the Birmingham Six. It was also Matthews, together with two other officers, who claimed in June 1984 that an accountant, Mr Malcolm Herring, had admitted his part in a conspiracy to commit arson. Mr Herring maintained that, following legal advice, his only response to their questions was to give his name, address and date of birth.

The statement containing the alleged admission was not signed by Mr Herring. Matthews explained in court that the absence of a signature was due to the fact that he had not requested Mr Herring to sign the document on the grounds that, when asked to sign statements, it is quite usual for prisoners to tear them up. The station sergeant agreed under cross-examination, however, that there was simply insufficient time for Mr Herring to have made the admissions attributed to him. Indeed, Herring had spent just three minutes in the CID room when he was supposed to have confessed. Mr Herring was acquitted by the jury (see Appendix B).

Matthews has since been required to resign from the force for refusing to obey an order returning him to uniformed duty, although West Midlands police have stated that this order was not made as a result of his operational activities. Before his resignation Matthews claimed to have obtained another incriminating, but disputed, statement from a Mr Martin Foran in respect of a robbery committed in the early hours of 9th September 1984. When questioned about his whereabouts prior to his arrest, Foran replied that he had been shopping and pointed to two bags of mincemeat which he had recently purchased. The existence of the mincemeat was even recorded on Foran's custody sheet at the police station to which he was subsequently taken, where the duty inspector asked Mr Foran's legal adviser to deliver the bags to Mr Foran's wife, Valerie. Strangely, however, Matthews and his colleagues steadfastly denied in evidence that Foran had any meat or other shopping with him in his car when they arrested him. Foran was convicted and sentenced to eight years' imprisonment.

We know of a number of disputed confessions allegedly obtained by officers who seem to have worked with each other on an occasional basis only. Of course, the possibility that such complaints may be false and/or malicious cannot be discounted; however it must be emphasised (see page 18) that all the complaints received by the inquiry team had been recorded in writing soon after each defendant's arrest, so that they could not have been dreamt up later in response to any adverse publicity about the Squad. There is some cause , therefore, to doubt the credibility of the evidence given by Squad officers in cases besides those outlined above where defendants have steadfastly alleged that statements attributed to them in police custody are the creation of Squad detectives.

Time and location of interviews

A recurring theme in the complaints to us about the conduct of the Serious Crime Squad has been that families and friends did not know where those arrested by Squad officers had been taken. It was claimed on several occasions that the officers were reluctant to impart this information, and that there was no other way of discovering the destination of those arrested. The situation of Mrs Julie McCabe, whose daughter Eileen had been arrested by the Squad in 1987, is an example:

> By now I was becoming very worried so I ran next door to my neighbour Mrs Parkes who had a telephone and rang Bradford Street Police Station. They said they knew nothing about Eileen McCabe. I then rang Bordesley Green Police Station who told me to try Stechford. I rang Stechford Police Station and again I was told that they didn't know Eileen McCabe but the lady officer who spoke to me said she would find out where she was ... I left it at that and believed they would ring back but in fact they never did.

Eileen had, in fact, been at Bradford Street police station all day. When she was brought to trial she was acquitted on the direction of the judge because her contact with her solicitor had been delayed.

It might have been expected that Squad detectives would take those arrested to the building at which the Squad was based. Such an assumption would, however, be misplaced. Before 1986 the Squad was based at force headquarters at Lloyd House in Birmingham City Centre, where there are apparently no custody or interviewing facilities. Detectives therefore made use of whichever police station they found convenient.

In 1986 the Squad moved its base to Bradford Street police station. But Eileen McCabe was one of the very few people whose cases we have researched who was interviewed at Bradford Street. Indeed, there appears to have been no particular pattern as to where an interview took place.

This lack of knowledge on the part of the suspect's relatives and friends as to his or her whereabouts would obviously make it difficult to arrange externally for any legal representation for anyone held in custody by the Squad. The refusal to tell the suspects themselves where they were being taken would, of course, increase their own feelings of isolation and disorientation.

The apparently haphazard selection of interviewing venues also had the effect of alienating a number of divisional officers, whether in uniform or CID, who found their own workplace disrupted by a clique of outside officers who insisted on taking control. Since the Squad routinely denied a suspect access to a solicitor (see below) custody officers, in particular, were often placed in a very difficult position.

The Squad effected many of its arrests in the early hours of the morning. This was also a favoured time for subsequent interrogations. Hassan Khan, for example, was supposed to have been interviewed in a car at 2am. Of the arrests which we have considered, approximately 80 percent were made early in the morning between the hours of 5.15am and 9am; 60 percent between 5.15am and 8am. This is normal police practice in order both to ensure that suspects are at home and to prevent their being alerted by their family. Nevertheless, one side-effect of arresting and interrogating suspects at such times would have been that interviewees would be suffering from at least some loss of sleep. This would make them substantially weaker in a psychological sense, and therefore somewhat less likely to be able to resist the rigours of police questioning.

Police officers also need their sleep. If members of the Serious Crime Squad were working these hours as a matter of routine overtime (as we believe) and not because of well-managed shift patterns, it is inevitable that such practice would have had a deleterious effect on Squad efficiency.

Denial of access to a solicitor

Under section 58(1) of PACE:

> A person arrested and held in custody in a police station or other premises shall be entitled, if he so requests, to consult a solicitor privately at any time.

When someone has been arrested on reasonable suspicion of having committed a 'serious arrestable offence' the police have a discretion under section 58(8) of PACE to delay access to a solicitor for up to 36 hours if they believe, *inter alia*, that this may alert other suspects or in any way hinder the recovery of stolen property. A large number of people arrested by the Squad were denied access on these grounds. In fact, apart from the few cases in which solicitors were not requested, the police delayed access in *every* case submitted to us except one. It seems that anyone detained by the Serious Crime Squad who requested the presence of a solicitor had access delayed as a matter of routine. Section 58(6) requires that delay be authorised by an officer of at least the rank of superintendent: custody records submitted to us show that Superintendent Michael Holder gave that authority in eight cases.

Such delay in obtaining access to a solicitor was highly significant. Research carried out for the Royal Commission on Criminal Procedure (Irving and Hildendorf, 1981) found that very few interviewees possessed the 'iron will' to remain silent under questioning in the absence of a solicitor, and this was borne out by our own investigations. On the other hand, we found that no incriminating statements were made when a solicitor was present, and the Squad carried out remarkably few interrogations after the defendant's legal representative had arrived at the police station. Indeed, the Squad usually claimed to have obtained a confession from the suspect by the time a solicitor arrived at the relevant police station, so that there would be little need for further questioning. Moreover, once a suspect had made damaging admissions, the next logical step would be to charge them. Interrogating suspects about a crime for which they have already been charged is in breach of paragraph 17.5 of the PACE Code of Practice on the detention, treatment and questioning of persons by the police unless it is 'necessary' or 'in the interests of justice'.

It might be assumed by a lay person that if an admission is obtained by the police after they have unlawfully denied a suspect access to a solicitor, then the trial judge would automatically rule such evidence inadmissible in court. This would, of course, have the effect of rendering the admission(s) virtually useless as far as the prosecution is concerned. But that is not the present legal position. In fact, as was pointed out in Chapter Three, section 78(1) of PACE gives the judge a discretion to refuse to admit any evidence (including an alleged confession) if that evidence has been unlawfully obtained, whilst under section

76 of PACE the judge may be satisfied that the confession is not 'unreliable' even though the requirements of PACE and the Codes have not been strictly complied with.

In practice, judges often allow such evidence. We are aware of only one case brought by the Squad - that of Eileen McCabe - where evidence was excluded on the grounds that access to a solicitor had been improperly delayed. A particular reason for this decision was that Ms McCabe had great difficulty in both reading and writing, and therefore could not understand what had been recorded by the interviewing officers during her interrogation.

The Court of Appeal case of *R v Samuel* (discussed in Chapter Three) was, in fact, concerned with the interrogation of a suspect by West Midlands police officers, but the ruling does not seem to have affected the practices disclosed by the cases we have examined. Whenever a suspect requested the presence of a solicitor, this was usually delayed at least until the detectives felt able to claim that they had obtained a confession from the interviewee. Indeed, it is a common practice in police forces nationwide for police officers to interrogate suspects 'informally' when their solicitors are not present, so that there are no checks either on the propriety of what happens or on the accuracy of what is reported. (Sanders and Bridges, 1990.) Of the cases we have examined we know of only one - in September 1981 - in which the suspect's solicitor was permitted to attend an interrogation before any confession had been obtained. In this particular case, and following his solicitor's advice, almost every response to questions asked of the suspect was recorded as 'no reply'.

The defendant in question was Mr Ronald (Ronnie) Brown. He was a member of the notorious Thursday Gang (see Chapter Two) whose activities were the focus of Operation Cat. Indeed, Ronnie Brown was named as one of Britain's most wanted men in 1966 when he and eight other prisoners, including John McVicar, escaped from a coach taking them back to Parkhurst Prison on the Isle of Wight. Described in 1968 by Judge Mervyn Griffiths-Jones as a 'potential murderer', he was undoubtedly one of the most important criminals successfully prosecuted on the basis of Squad evidence. He received a sentence of 18 years' imprisonment. It should be noted that Brown's case is a clear example of the fact that it is perfectly possible to allow a serious criminal access to immediate legal representation and still obtain a conviction.

It was not always necessary for the Squad to make a formal decision as to whether to permit a suspect to have contact with a solicitor. We have examined a number of cases where the suspect himself signed his custody record to the effect that he did not want to see a solicitor. In many of these cases it has been claimed that this decision was not made voluntarily and, in effect, was simply an unlawful Squad method of denying such access without the need for the decision to be authorised by a senior officer. It has been shown by research commissioned by the Lord Chancellor's Department that this practice is not confined to the West Midlands force. In all the police forces researched, some police officers unlawfully denied access to a few suspects but 'doctored' the custody records to make it appear otherwise (Sanders *et al*, 1989, ch. 4; Sanders and Bridges, 1990).

We return again to the case of George Glen Lewis, who in January 1987 was arrested by DS Reynolds and DC Perkins of the Serious Crime Squad on suspicion of robbery. After he was taken to Wednesfield police station - where he was allegedly subjected to both verbal and physical abuse and then presented with a custody record sheet - Lewis told his solicitor that:

> Perkins told me to sign a blank part of the sheet about seeing a Solicitor. He told me to sign my name first and I knew that he would cross out the part "I do want to see a Solicitor" leaving the words "I do not want to see a Solicitor". I then started to cross out the line "I do not want to see a Solicitor" and when he saw me doing

this he suddenly knocked the pen out of my hand and said "just fucking sign there", pointing to the space for my signature.

Mr Lewis's custody record shows that it is the line requesting the presence of a solicitor which has been deleted. However, it also bears a line through the words 'I do not' which are the first three words in the sentence 'I do not want a solicitor at this time'. Having reached the word 'not', the line suddenly veers off at 90 degrees towards the bottom of the page. Moreover, Mr Lewis had already spoken to his solicitor by telephone and requested that he come to the police station as soon as possible. It is, perhaps, significant that this call was made in the presence of the duty custody sergeant at a time when Messrs Reynolds and Perkins were in another part of the building. Mr Lewis still has seven years of his ten-year sentence to run.

DC Perkins was also involved in the case of Mr Charles Campbell, who had been arrested in 1985 on suspicion of armed robbery. An identification parade took place between 11.15 am and 11.30 am on 27th March 1985. The presiding officer, Detective Chief Inspector Bob Morris, then spoke to Mr Campbell's solicitor, Mr Shipley (himself a 'former eminent police officer', according to the judge), who left once it had been agreed that there should be 'no interviews unless solicitor present'. Mr Morris recorded precisely these words on a sheet of paper. He also noted: 'Left Station 11.45 am'. Yet according to Messrs Perkins and Rawlings, Campbell confessed to them within a quarter of an hour of Morris's departure.

These were the sort of situations referred to by the Police Complaints Authority in its 1989 Annual Report:

> However in serious criminal cases there is a temptation for detective officers, who are trying to solve a serious crime, to pay less than full attention to the Codes of Practice when dealing with suspects in custody. There are two different interests at play: on the one hand there is the custody officer who is trained to follow strictly the Codes of Practice while on the other the detective's interest is to extract information from the detained suspect and to prove his case. The two interests are not easily reconciled. The detective may be inclined to think in these circumstances that the codes are administrative guidance. They are a great deal more than that for section 67(8) of the Act states that failure to comply with the codes is a disciplinary offence. (para. 3.5.)

'Plastic-baggings'

'Plastic-bagging' is a term coined by the media. It has been used to describe the allegation by five men arrested by the Serious Crime Squad that they had had some sort of plastic bag put over their heads by police officers until they were about to pass out in order either to force them to confess to a given crime, or to sign a statement of a confession which the police had already prepared.

The first allegation of this nature was made in 1980 by Mr George Keith Twitchell, who was arrested in 1980 and charged with the murder of a Securicor Guard. Mr Twitchell subsequently submitted voluntarily to a lie detector test under the supervision of Professor Canning, an expert in forensic medicine, and was injected with sodium amytal (a so-called 'truth drug') in front of witnesses. After these tests Professor Canning concluded that he felt inclined to believe Mr Twitchell's account, but this evidence was ruled inadmissible in court. On 22nd February 1982 Twitchell was found guilty of robbery and manslaughter, for which he was sentenced to 15 and 20 years' imprisonment respectively.

Four further allegations of 'plastic-baggings' were made in 1982-83 by some of those arrested as a result of Operation Cat. Mr Harry Derek Tredaway claimed to have suffered a number of injuries as a result of his alleged assault and was examined soon afterwards by a Home Office pathologist, who concluded:

> In the case of Mr Tredaway, the finding of petechial haemorrhages on the shoulder and on the front of the chest is exactly where I would expect to find them if a plastic bag had been held over his head in the manner he described... Furthermore, the finding of abrasions of the mucous membrane inside the right corner of the mouth is fully consistent with the statement of the complainant that hands were put over his mouth.

Mr Tredaway brought a civil action for alleged assault against West Midlands police, but it was struck out by a county court district registrar in August 1990 on the grounds that Tredaway and his lawyers had allowed too much time to elapse between bringing the claim to court and first giving notice that they intended to do so (in 1987).

Each of the defendants who made allegations of 'plastic-bagging' was convicted, and there is little objective evidence supporting their complaints. The inquiry team is also unaware of any such allegations being made after 1983. If these complaints had been made in respect of the activities either of another force or of a different squad or division within the West Midlands force, we should therefore have remained distinctly sceptical. In the light of the other evidence of alleged malpractice within the Serious Crime Squad, however, allegations of 'plastic-baggings' - which may have seemed far-fetched to many who heard them when they were first made public - must be viewed with hindsight as a cause for concern.

Other physical violence

We have received some complaints alleging other physical violence by the Serious Crime Squad in an attempt to force the suspect either to confess or to sign a statement of confession written by Squad officers. Such allegations were, of course, crucial to the case of the recently-exonerated Birmingham Six. Many of these complaints were made by others arrested at the same time as those complaining of 'plastic-baggings'. From about 1986, onwards, however, there are significantly fewer complaints of physical violence during arrests and interrogations.

It has been suggested to us by a number of known criminals that the reason for this reduction is that few detectives would now contemplate physical assault, because it is both counter-productive (in that it allows defendants to call medical evidence to buttress their cases), and also because nowadays interviewing techniques are so sophisticated in their application of psychological pressure that they can achieve the desired results equally well. We have insufficient evidence on which to judge the accuracy of this claim.

A case which nevertheless causes us some concern is that of Mr Derek Boswell, who, on 4th May 1983, was arrested on suspicion of robbery and taken to Bridge Street police station. After he refused to make a statement, but while still in the custody of Squad officers,

Boswell says that someone burst into the room and punched him several times in the face and the ribs, shouting 'Rob old women will you? You'll make a statement, you bastard.'

Approximately ten hours after this alleged attack Boswell was examined by Dr Clive Joseph Bruton, a general medical practitioner. He formed the view at the time that Boswell was:

> a plethoric man and there were recent blood stains on his yellow tee shirt and green trousers. Examination of the face showed slight bruising and swelling of the left cheek underneath the left eye and the nose was slightly swollen. Internal examination of the nostril confirmed the presence of recent blood clot in the Little's area of both nostrils.... the injuries to his face and nose were minor in character but there had obviously been some bleeding from both nostrils. The injuries could also be compatible with the alleged history of several blows to the face.

The officer allegedly responsible has never been identified, although Mr Boswell has given a description of him. Boswell was convicted and sentenced to three years' imprisonment.

On 1st November 1983 DS Brian Morton, who had served on the Squad from March 1973 until February 1976, was convicted of assaulting a suspect occasioning actual bodily harm; he was sentenced to twelve months' imprisonment (six months suspended for two years) and was dismissed from the force at disciplinary proceedings conducted three days later. (Two detective constables who had never been members of the Squad were convicted on similar charges and given nine months' imprisonment, half of which was suspended for two years. They too subsequently dismissed from the force.) Police Cadet Adrian Dart, who had become an outcast within the force after testifying against his colleagues, resigned from the force four months later.

Threatening suspects

Whilst the number of complaints received by the inquiry team alleging actual physical violence by Squad officers on suspects declined significantly in relation to incidents after 1986, there was a corresponding increase in the number of allegations that suspects or witnesses were threatened in some way by members of the Serious Crime Squad. There has also been a number of recent court cases in which evidence adduced by the Squad has been ruled inadmissible because of such threats (see Appendix B). The most recent occurred in January 1990, when the prosecution was forced to drop charges of robbery against Mr Harry Allan because it was found that DC David Woodley had subjected the main prosecution witness to unlawful duress. A co-defendant who pleaded guilty also declined to give evidence against Mr Allan.

Coincidentally the same judge, Malcolm Potter, also presided at the trial of Mr Paul Fitzsimmons in October 1988. Fitzsimmons was alleged by DS McManus and DC Adams to have confessed to the robbery of a florist's, but this admission was found to have been extracted under duress. Thus the judge directed an acquittal and announced that he was writing to Chief Constable Geoffrey Dear asking him to clear up doubts about McManus's credibility.

Fitzsimmons later alleged that McManus had visited him on remand in Winson Green Prison and threatened to re-arrest him on release unless he agreed to give evidence for the prosecution against Mr Ronnie Bolden (a Squad case concerning an alleged armed robbery). Fitzsimmons maintains that he was told to say that the solicitors acting for Mr Bolden, Saunders & Co., had attempted to bribe him to give evidence for their own client. McManus did indeed make just such an allegation about Saunders & Co. when the case first came to court in October 1988, and he produced the prison visitors' book ostensibly to prove that two representatives of the firm had been present at the relevant date and time.

The two men in question, Messrs James Montgomery and Paul Baker, did have an appointment with Fitzsimmons at that time, and had each submitted a signed application to the prison authorities for a pass, known as a Visitor's Order, to enable them to enter the prison for that purpose. However, Mr Baker had been called away at the last minute to deal with another client in Golders Green police station in London, and therefore could not possibly have been in Winson Green on the same day. Yet signatures of *both* men were recorded in the visitors' book as having visited the prison (see Chapter Five). McManus admitted in evidence that he had been the subject of a number of complaints of alleged fabrication of evidence, and that he had been investigated six times in the previous five years. At a re-trial in June 1989 - ordered because of McManus's allegations - Mr Bolden was acquitted. He had spent 22 months on remand in custody.

Hassan Khan, whose conviction for armed robbery was quashed in February 1990, has also consistently claimed that he was threatened by Squad officers. During the journey from his arrest in North Wales to his arrival in Birmingham, Mr Khan alleges that he was threatened with physical abuse and warned about what would happen to him at at Chelmsley Wood police station. He also alleges that he was told of what happened to the Birmingham Six and how they would get a confession from him in the same way. He was apparently told that he was going to meet a very important man who dealt with the Birmingham bombers.

Mr Albert McCabe also claims to have been threatened. Arrested on suspicion of robbery, he turned supergrass (see next chapter) in 1 986. Four complainants have stated they were implicated in certain offences by McCabe's evidence. Later that year, however, he sent a letter to the solicitors representing all those whom he had implicated. In it he claimed that he had given his statements under duress from officers of the Serious Crime Squad, and because they had told him that he would otherwise be sentenced to 18 years' imprisonment. He also admitted to lying in court. He was not produced in court as a prosecution witness thereafter. One of those whom he had implicated, Mr Hassan Khan, had his conviction quashed by the Court of Appeal in February 1990.

Mr McCabe's sister, Eileen, was also apparently the victim of undue pressure by the Squad. She was arrested in 1987 on suspicion of participation in an armed robbery. Although it was agreed that her children (aged four and five) could be looked after by their grandmother, they were all taken to Bradford Street police station. The children were, however, taken to a different cell while Ms McCabe was interrogated. She was denied access to a solicitor, and at the conclusion of the interview signed a document purporting to be a contemporaneous note of what had been said. It contained incriminating statements. At her trial it was maintained on her behalf that she had been so worried about what was happening to her children that her interrogation amounted to oppressive conduct by the Squad. Moreover, evidence was adduced at the trial that Ms McCabe had the greatest difficulty in reading, so that she could not have fully understood the implications of what she was signing. Judge Potter therefore excluded the alleged confession on the grounds that it had been obtained unfairly. The prosecution was therefore unable to proceed.

Another complainant, Mr Raymond Fryer, alleges that during his interrogation in

1986 for alleged robbery, 'every time I asked about my daughter they said they would put her in care...'

George Glen Lewis, perhaps, makes the most startling allegation. He claims that in January 1987 he was threatened with a hypodermic syringe in order to make him sign blank sheets of paper. The signed statements contain incriminating admissions to armed robbery for which he was subsequently convicted and sentenced to ten years' imprisonment.

It is noteworthy that all these cases involved incidents alleged to have occurred after the introduction of PACE, which was supposed to prevent them. If the allegations are true, it follows that PACE is seriously defective.

Implicating co-accused

In law, an alleged confession is evidence only against its maker, but in agreeing with the account given by the confessor, the other suspects make it evidence against themselves. The police are therefore absolved from the need actually to prove any other link between suspects who implicate themselves in this way and the crime in question. It is not even necessary to obtain a complete confession from each defendant outlining his or her role in the crime: the confession given by the original confessor is treated as evidence against co-defendants who express their agreement with the statement because their agreement is taken to be an adoption of the confession as if it were their own.

The inquiry team is aware of five Serious Crime Squad cases where brief admissions were apparently made. We should point out that it is perfectly proper for police officers to rely on evidence obtained in this way, but we do feel that the fact that such evidence is admissible in court represents an important defect in the law. The following one-line admissions were thus all used against those alleged to have uttered the words in question.

When told that his co-defendant Mr Cartwright had implicated him, Mr Geoffrey Cheetham, for example, is alleged to have said : 'Yes, but I ain't saying nothing.'

When Derek Boswell was told that he had been implicated by his co-accused John Brett, Squad officers allege he replied:

> The fucking bastard, I'll kill him.... Look Sergeant, we all decided not to make statements if we were caught and I can't make one against my own son, can I?

Martin Foran's response to being told that his co-accused had made a statement implicating him was, claims the detective: 'What can I say? It's all there, isn't it?' And David McCabe's reply to the news that his brother Albert had implicated him is alleged to have been: 'Yes, he hasn't missed much.'

In none of these four cases did the defendant who was allegedly admitting to taking part in crime actually sign the notes taken by the interviewing policemen. In the fifth case of this type, Gordon Chakki did sign the record because, he says, he was confused and frightened (see below). It contained the admission, 'Yes, it's all down there as it happened.' All five defendants claim that the admissions in question were fabricated by Squad officers, but all were convicted. But whoever was the author of each of these admissions, these incidents clearly highlight the legal defect which may create a temptation for some police officers to fabricate one-line admissions - lacking in any detail - as a substitute for further investigation.

Confessions in a Squad car

We have noted that a number of alleged confessions were obtained by the Serious Crime Squad in the course of interviews carried out in a police car. This is a particularly difficult area, since the PACE Codes of Practice offer little specific guidance as to the conduct of such interviews, whilst the Judges Rules contained no such guidance at all.

One admission allegedly made in such circumstances was that of Hassan Khan (see above), but its veracity was doubted by the Court of Appeal. Moreover, DS Swinnerton, DC Rawlings and DC Howkins all alleged that Mr Khan confessed to robbing a Dixons store on 12th September 1987, despite the fact that the thief had run away from the store (discharging a shotgun), at a time when Mr Khan was physically incapable of running because he had had two of his toes amputated only a week before.

Mr John Edwards was alleged by DS Owen and DC Woodley to have made a 'car seat confession' to armed robbery between 11.10pm and 12 midnight on 10th November 1987 while he was being driven from Salford (where he was arrested) to Stechford police station in Birmingham. Mr Edwards claimed to have been driven aimlessly around Birmingham the following day, during which time DS Bowen, DC Quin and DC Woodley claimed that he made further incriminating admissions. Edwards maintained that both interviews were fabricated by the officers concerned after he had been improperly denied access to a solicitor. Although the prosecution accepted the latter submission, the judge ruled the alleged confessions to be admissible evidence, and Edwards was convicted. He was sentenced to 14 years' imprisonment. He was, however, given leave to appeal in 1990 despite the lapse of time, and in January 1991 the Court of Appeal quashed his conviction.

The inquiry team is of the opinion that Squad officers misinterpreted the requirement in section 30 of PACE (that where a person is arrested for an offence he should be taken to a police station as soon as practicable after the arrest). This section does not allow police officers a discretion to use a police station of their choice. Since it was 'practicable' to have taken both Hassan Khan and John Edwards to a police station in the vicinity of their arrests, the police should not have delayed taking Messrs Khan and Edwards to a police station until they were back in the West Midlands. On the contrary, Khan should have been taken to a police station in or near Caernarvon, whilst Edwards should have been taken to one in or around Salford. The failure of the police to comply with the requirements of section 30 meant that the men arrested were denied the protection of other aspects of PACE and COP including, for example, the right to request legal advice. Paragraph 6.3 of COP, for example, would have ruled out any interviews in a Squad car before arrival at the chosen police station in the West Midlands if Squad officers had decided not to begin the interrogation of Khan and Edwards in Carnarvon or Salford police stations.

In one of the many cases which resulted from Operation Cat, which was carried out by a combination of officers from the Serious Crime Squad and No. 4 Regional Crime Squad, Mr John Patrick Irvine was convicted of robbery and manslaughter in February 1982 on the basis of a car seat confession allegedly obtained from him in January 1981 - i.e. before the introduction of PACE - by two regional detectives. Irvine received concurrent prison sentences of 15 years and 20 years respectively. He claims, however, that the admissions were fabricated by the officers, one of whom was later recruited by the Serious Crime Squad.

Fabrication of confessions

In every one of the Serious Crime Squad cases which has been submitted to this inquiry, it has been alleged that officers from the Serious Crime Squad concocted statements from the suspects which contained, at the very least, some incriminating admissions and more often, a full confession. According to police records, most of the disputed interviews lasted between 35 minutes and two hours: this appears to be of no particular significance.

The important feature is that in every complainant's trial the alleged confession or admission formed the cornerstone of the prosecution's evidence: in many cases an uncorroborated and disputed confession was the sum total of the Crown's evidence. In the cases of William Barrett *et al* in 1986, John Bullivant *et al* in 1987, Robert Burston *et al* in 1988, and Ronnie Bolden in 1989, evidence claimed by the prosecution to corroborate an alleged confession was found to be false (see Chapter Five).

Without being able to inspect certain important documents, either because they have been shredded by West Midlands police - in accordance with their former practice (see Chapter Six) - or because we have been denied access to them by the same force or by the Police Complaints Authority, it is, of course, impossible for us to adjudicate conclusively on the truth or otherwise of each individual accusation. If the complaints are considered as a whole, however, there appear to be several characteristics common to many of the allegations. Since it is true both that most of the complainants were not acquainted with one another and also that the allegations before us cover a ten-year period up to 1989, we find this disturbing. The specific detail of this pattern of complaints has been dealt with earlier in this chapter. But we should also like to make some more general points.

The sheer scale of the complaints received has been remarkable. Of course we recognise fully both that the Serious Crime Squad was detailed to apprehend serious 'professional' criminals, and that the latter would, in turn, be very likely to take every possibility of discrediting those seeking to apprehend them. We have therefore been mindful of the fact that only a very few complainants had no criminal record (excluding motoring offences, about which we have not enquired) before coming into contact with Squad officers. Most complainants had a string of convictions which often included burglary, robbery and associated offences.

It is to be expected that such experienced defendants would know that any admissions made during the course of a police interview can be used as evidence in a court of law, whether or not the alleged author agrees to sign the alleged written record of them. Indeed , our experience of interviewing defendants with previous convictions suggests that they have a knowledge of criminal procedure of which even a legal practitioner would be proud. Such defendants would be unlikely to forget this knowledge even if, as is alleged on almost every occasion, Squad officers failed both to explain the reason for their arrest or to caution suspects as required by PACE (or, before 1986, by the Judges Rules) before commencing interrogation. Yet we have seen a striking number of depositions by Squad officers stating that the accused made a full or partial confession which they then refused to sign when it was presented to them.

We have also been very surprised that so many defendants apparently confessed so readily. Again we would have expected that those with previous experience of police interrogation techniques would have been substantially less likely to admit to criminal activity than appears to have been the case. The Lord Chief Justice, Lord Lane, made the very same point when on 23rd February 1990 he announced the quashing of the convictions of Mr Hassan Khan for robbery and wounding with intent.

A disturbing feature common to many of the interview records we have seen is the scant amount of detail contained in the alleged confessions. If any detail is recorded, it is frequently confined to the names of alleged accomplices. Thus, in an interview which took only 26 minutes in total, Mr Carlton Alladice's alleged confession to robbery (see above, p. 45) was simply:

> You know what happened at the post office. We went behind the counter and took the money. That's what you want to hear. I've told you my part now.

Alladice was refused access to a solicitor for eight hours. He continues to deny that he ever confessed at all, and claims that his alleged admission was pure fabrication on the part of DS Swinnerton and DC Rawlings, who had been involved in the unsuccessful prosecution of John Bullivant and others (see above, p. 43 and Appendix B). He was convicted on 3rd April 1987 and sentenced to eight years' imprisonment. Despite ruling that the police had acted illegally in denying him a solicitor, the Court of Appeal allowed Alladice's confession to stand and upheld his conviction.

Another unsigned, patchy confession was apparently provided in May 1983 by Mr Derek Boswell after he had been arrested for alleged robbery. Two Squad officers claim that Boswell said: 'Look, I might as well tell you, it was me and John that had the money away, but Timmy wasn't there.'

Boswell made no other admissions.

We have also been struck by the similarity of the phraseology which occurs throughout the records of interviews which we have examined. Although one of the members of the inquiry team has a particular interest in linguistics, we should like to have submitted much of the material before us to an expert in this field for a more comprehensive analysis. We should especially have liked to know if it were possible that many of the alleged confessions could have been drawn from a common source. Unfortunately, a lack of time and sufficient funds have precluded the commissioning of such research, but we should certainly encourage and support such a project if sufficient funds and expertise should become available.

There are essentially three reasons for suggesting that such research be undertaken. One is concerned with detail. For example, upon being made aware of the charges against them in the interview in which an admission was allegedly obtained, the suspect frequently replied with a variant of one of the following phrases:

a)   'That's a bit heavy';
b)   'You're spot on';
c)   'That bastard's really put me in it'; or
d)   'You're putting a good case against me'.

As the interviewing officers told a suspect of the evidence they had against him, the reply 'I've got a lot to think about' also seems to occur with undue regularity. Moreover, Squad officers frequently recorded that suspects on the point of a confession 'smile'. This seems to the inquiry team to be a most unexpected reaction from so many people. We have also noticed that those actually confessing often prefaced their accounts with a phrase like 'I'll put my hands up'.

Secondly, there seems to be little difference - either in general patterns of speech or in specific colloquialisms - between the statements allegedly made by suspects no matter what their country or region of origin. Thus persons from Birmingham, the Black Country,

London, Manchester, Ireland and elsewhere seem to utter no distinctive slang during their interviews. Rarely, too, have we come across any distinctive speech characteristics in the statements, whether made by people of Caucasian, Caribbean or Asian origin, although some Afro-Caribbeans (whilst otherwise apparently talking like everyone else) were recorded as ending many clauses and sentences with the word 'man', as in 'I ain't done nothing, man'. One major exception to this is an interview with Mr Richard Taylor, who is recorded as having a quite distinctive manner of speaking.

We should not have been so concerned about these apparent similarities if the speech recorded had been more or less akin to so-called Oxford English for - although the record would still be inaccurate - this might suggest that the Squad note-taker had simply corrected any linguistic deficiencies on the part of the suspect. In fact, however, it appears to us that the recorded speech of both interviewer and interviewee is consistently in the same vernacular.

Thirdly, when reading the alleged records of the interviews in which confessions were obtained we have been struck by a general air of unreality. Although it is naturally difficult to do more than speculate about such issues - when the reader of a statement cannot be sure of such vital ingredients as the intonation of the speaker - we were, for example, conscious of the number of apparently sudden and unexplained changes of mood within the interview room. Trevor Campbell's floods of tears and his taking of DC Perkins's hand as a comforter (see above, p. 44) are, if true, perhaps the most notable instances of such behaviour.

Before leaving this section, we should mention what we consider to be an extraordinary anomaly in the procedure of the inquiry supervised by the Police Complaints Authority: it has decided that no complainant should be allowed a copy of his or her statement to the investigating West Yorkshire officers. Its justification for withholding this information is the case of *R v Makanjuola* (*Lexis*, 16th March 1989). *Makanjuola* was concerned with section 49 of the Police Act 1964, but this section is no longer part of the law. It was repealed by section 98(1)(a) of PACE, which makes it possible for the PCA to disclose information to persons 'for the proper discharge of the functions of the Authority'. It was thought by most observers that the purpose of this section was precisely to allow complainants to be kept informed of the progress of any subsequent investigation. Since the main allegation throughout the inquiry has been that police officers falsified statements, it is very worrying that complainants should be unable to check either the accuracy or veracity of what they are alleged to have said to the investigating authorities.

5

Other Patterns of Behaviour of the Serious Crime Squad

Fabrication of non-confession evidence

We have received few allegations of this nature, but the examples given here should, perhaps, be taken as warnings that forensic evidence is not necessarily infallible. The case of Ronnie Bolden (see Chapter Four and Appendix B) is, perhaps, the best known of those involving allegations that Serious Crime Squad officers falsified evidence other than confessions. It has not yet been established who was responsible for the alteration to the prison signing-in book (see p. 53).

A second remarkable feature about this case is the allegation by the defence that the police had attempted to fabricate forensic evidence to corroborate Mr Bolden's alleged confession by rubbing Mr Bolden's shoes and socks on the carpet of a getaway car. This is not unlike the defence allegation in the case of Robert Burston *et al* (see Appendix B), where it was alleged that police planted black plastic bin liners with the defendants' fingerprints on them - they had been handling refuse - in a post office van in order to incriminate them in the robbery of its contents. Bolden was acquitted by a jury, whilst charges against Burston and his fellow defendants were dropped.

Mr George Keith Twitchell alleges that there was an attempt to implicate him in a crime by planting some hair from a hairbrush brought to the police station by his wife. This 'evidence' was not used by the prosecution in court, however, when independent forensic analysis revealed the sample to be more like that provided for the test by Mrs Twitchell than that of Mr Twitchell.

Another well-known case is that of Martin Foran, who was convicted in 1985 of robbery on the basis of evidence gleaned by the Serious Crime Squad. After several requests to see documents relating to his client's case (in response to which he was told they had been shredded in accordance with force policy), solicitor Mark Phillips was shown two purported copies of Mr Foran's custody record in April 1990. One, however, had more entries recorded on it than the other, whilst entries relating to interviews with Foran had been altered

Supergrasses

Information is the lifeblood of specialist police units such as the Serious Crime Squad. Yet it is frequently difficult to obtain without the assistance of persons who are themselves known criminals. The police have an awkward task in maintaining what is an inherently uneasy relationship between themselves and their informants whilst at the same time ensuring that they are not seen to be condoning illegal behaviour.

Every specialist squad in any police force would therefore expect to have a number of informants who might provide them with useful information in return for a small monetary payment or a more sympathetic explanation for the informant's conduct in a criminal trial . There is no doubt that the Serious Crime Squad made use of a number of such informants. Indeed, almost all the Squad's arrests were initiated in this way: sometimes this information came from a co-defendant.

But in the last few years it has become clear (from answers given by police and prosecution witnesses under cross-examination) that a qualitatively different sort of informant has come to provide certain specialist units with much of their information. This is the so-called 'supergrass' or, as he is known in the West Midlands Police Annual Reports, the 'protected police informant' to whom, in return for information received, the police undertake to provide protection, a new identity and a new home in a distant location after the completion of the trial(s) at which he is to give evidence.

Before and during such trials, a protected informant is kept, for his own safety, in protective custody in a police cell. The closeness which results between the protected informant and the police makes it even more important that the police maintain the highest standards of propriety while investigating any allegations made by the informant.

As we have seen, a series of security van robberies took place in the early 1980s, involving the theft of thousands of pounds on each occasion. To combat these crimes, more than 50 detectives from the West Midlands Serious Crime Squad and the No. 4 Regional Crime Squad were seconded to take part in Operation Cat. Much of the operation resulted from information received from Mr Keith Morgan.

Keith William Morgan is believed to have been the first Midlands supergrass. He was given the status of a protected police informant in 1980 but jumped bail and is thought to have set up a drug smuggling ring in North Africa. He was extradited to face trial, but the Serious Crime Squad still agreed to give him a 'supergrass deal'. Morgan implicated a large number of persons in serious crimes in the region, including Messrs Tredaway and Pender, who allege that they were subsequently the victims of 'plastic-baggings'. At Birmingham Crown Court in 1982, Morgan admitted 20 offences including armed robbery, kidnapping, burglary and conspiracy to import illicit drugs. Despite his absconding while on bail, the judge was asked to treat Morgan lightly. Mr Justice Bush accepted this submission. Instead of receiving a likely sentence of around 14 years' imprisonment, Morgan was sent down for five years.

Morgan had earlier alleged that a Detective Sergeant Oliver Duggan (not a member of the Serious Crime Squad) had helped to plan some robberies and that he had demanded £1,700 from Morgan. The consequences of these allegations were summarised for this inquiry in a letter dated 30th May 1990 from the then Acting Chief Constable, Paul Leopold:

> The allegations made by Mr Morgan were thoroughly investigated by Detective Superintendent Owen of Merseyside Police. The file was referred to the Director of Public Prosecutions, who, following advice from Counsel, stated on 6 June 1983 that the evidence did not justify criminal proceedings against the officer.

> On 15 June 1983 the then Acting Deputy Chief Constable, Mr Tom Meffen, made the decision that there would be no further action taken against Detective Sergeant Duggan.

This raises two issues of the utmost gravity. Many people were convicted primarily on the basis of evidence from Keith Morgan. But the investigation into DS Duggan's alleged activities reveals that Morgan was a totally unreliable witness.

Secondly, Keith Morgan had alleged corruption on the part of DS Duggan well before the

Operation Cat cases came to trial. Yet the conclusion to Mr Owen's inquiry into these allegations was not announced until some months afterwards. It should certainly have been possible either to expedite Mr Owen's investigation or to postpone the trial until it had been completed. It is therefore a matter of great concern that neither option was taken, since it is possible that the juries' verdicts would have been different had they known of the inquiry's outcome.

Mr Richard Mackay, who was arrested as part of Operation Cat, also turned supergrass. Nicknamed 'Mad Mac', he admitted in court in June 1983 that while in protective custody he had been taken drinking in the Eagles Basketball Club in West Bromwich by officers from the Serious Crime Squad. His evidence also implicated, among others, Tredaway and Pender. After confessing to 20 offences of armed robbery, he was jailed in March 1984 for just five years by Mr Justice Bush.

The 1987 Annual Report of the Chief Constable of the West Midlands Police officially disclosed what had by then been known by local criminals and crime reporters for some time. It said:

> The [Serious Crime] Squad has direct responsibility for the handling of protected police informants. The results achieved are very satisfactory. One series of trials recently concluded obtained convictions and substantial terms of imprisonment were imposed upon professional criminals for serious armed robberies including the use and in some cases discharge of firearms.

It is, however, noteworthy that on almost every occasion when Squad supergrass statements were used, the only corroborative evidence offered by the prosecution was an unsigned and disputed admission by the accused.

Moreover, we believe that the extract quoted above refers to evidence given by Mr Albert McCabe, who turned supergrass in 1986. Mr John Edwards, whose conviction for armed robbery on the basis of a disputed confession was quashed (see Appendix B), says that in November 1987 DC Owen used McCabe as an example of how giving evidence against robbers would make things go better for Edwards in court. McCabe gave the police over 100 names of persons who, he alleged, had been involved in burglaries, robberies and associated offences. They included that of Hassan Khan, who has now been cleared, and Javhed Akhtar and Tracy Evans, who were acquitted in the Crown Court. McCabe pleaded guilty to all 72 charges against him (as all supergrasses inevitably must in order to maintain some credibility) and was sentenced to six years' imprisonment. The charges brought by the prosecution were three of robbery, four of having a firearm with intent to commit robbery, one of attempted robbery and one of wounding. McCabe asked for 63 other offences (including two more armed robberies) to be taken into account.

Afterwards Mr McCabe says that he had many visits from Squad officers. Nevertheless, he refused to testify in further prosecutions. He then sent a letter to solicitors acting for the persons whom he had implicated, saying that he was now frightened for his life. He explained that his statements were made under duress from officers of the Serious Crime Squad. He alleges that a senior officer said that unless McCabe made the statements required by the police he would receive 18 years' imprisonment.

McCabe further admitted to having given perjured evidence in court, and to having been offered inducements by the police to do so. Apparently he was paid £10 per week, and he says that he was offered a further £25 if he gave evidence in court. Payment of £25 was received by him on 23rd December 1987 by Recorded Delivery No. F332733.

Mr McCabe also alleged that a Squad officer bought him a tracksuit for £56 and training shoes for £30 on condition that he gave evidence at court. He was also allowed to sleep with his wife every night in his cell at Chelmsley Wood police station and was provided with a television and alcoholic liquor.

While enjoying supergrass status, McCabe escaped from police custody. We have been given two purported explanations about the manner of his escape from protective custody at Chelmsley Wood police station, where all Squad informants were held. One version is that he simply walked through open doors. The other is that he absconded when Squad officers took him out for a curry. McCabe was re-arrested at a blues party after virtually the entire Squad had been taken off other duties to find him. No record of his escape was, however, logged in police records.

Paul Joseph Jarvis was another supergrass. He was arrested by the Squad after he and two other men carried out an unsuccessful robbery at a Kwiksave supermarket. He approached the Squad about doing a 'deal' with him to get bail: his real intention was to provide misleading information and then double-cross the police by jumping bail. This he did, but he was re-captured after a robbery in Devon. Back in Birmingham he made a genuine agreement to become a protected informant, and was held in police custody for eight months. Again, he was provided with a television, supplied with alcoholic liquor, and his girlfriend was allowed to sleep with him in his cell. Jarvis also claims to have been taken by Squad officers for a drink in a number of pubs.

Jarvis not only supplied the Serious Crime Squad with a long list of alleged criminals, he also admitted to taking part in an extraordinary number of crimes himself. The Annual Report for 1988 put it thus:

> A considerable amount of time is spent by officers handling protected police informants. One of whom currently being dealt with, has admitted responsibility for 1,500 offences in this Force area. *(sic)*.

Such admissions would, of course, assist the Squad's official, published detection rate.

After assisting the police in this way, Paul Jarvis was tried at Lincoln Crown Court where he admitted 17 crimes including armed robberies, aggravated burglaries and a contract shooting. He did, indeed, ask for a further 1,510 offences of burglary, aggravated burglary and armed robbery to be taken into account. Describing Jarvis as at the 'top of the second division in crime', Judge Geoffrey Jones sentenced him to just four years' imprisonment. He served only 16 months before being released.

However, at the trial of Gerry and Ronald Gall in August 1989, Judge Richard Curtis accepted that Jarvis could not possibly have committed all the offences which he had asked at his own trial to be taken into account, since he had been in prison at the time some of the offences had allegedly taken place. The judge went on to brand Jarvis a 'compulsive liar'. Nevertheless, both defendants were convicted by the jury on the basis of his evidence.

Finally, there is the case of Paul Bernard Charles Smith. On 23rd April 1984 Mr Don Davies, a garage owner from Shifnal near Wolverhampton, was battered to death by robbers who stole the weekend's takings of around £3,000. Divisional detectives investigating the case told the local *Express and Star* newspaper that someone had broken into Mr Davies's house and that there were signs of a fierce struggle.

On 24th May 1984, Smith was arrested and charged with Mr Davies's murder. Thirteen months later he was jailed for just six years for manslaughter. The prosecution accepted that

Smith had attempted to restrain his accomplice, Frank Gwilliam, from punching and kicking Mr Davies when he realised that the latter was an asthmatic. However, Mr Rudy Narayan, counsel for Mr Gwilliam, said that Smith had transferred responsibility for his own role in the event onto the shoulders of Gwilliam. He further alleged that Smith had suffered two black eyes while attacking Mr Davies and had deliberately started a fight the next day in order to account for his injuries.

Smith already had a criminal record for offences with violence, and he asked for another 74 offences - including two robberies, two aggravated burglaries and two burglaries - to be taken into consideration. Gwilliam had no previous convictions for violence. The judge said that he approached Smith's version of events 'with great caution'. Yet Gwilliam was sentenced to ten years' imprisonment.

One explanation for Mr Justice Tucker's leniency towards Smith was that the latter was said by the prosecution to be providing information which was proving a 'windfall' for the police. Smith admitted in court that the police would 'look after' his family and help him find a job on his release from prison, but he denied being offered £5,000 and a new identity. Detective Chief Inspector John McCammont of Telford police agreed in court that while in police custody, Smith had a colour television and video recorder, was taken drinking in police clubs under escort, went to a nightclub once under escort and had regular visits from his family. He also said that Smith's family had been provided with a new home.

The group to whom he was allegedly supplying information was the Serious Crime Squad.

Missing papers

A police officer's notebook must be countersigned by a senior officer at regular intervals. It must be kept in a safe place for a minimum of seven years, and the loss of such a notebook is a disciplinary offence. Seven such notebooks containing records of interviews and movements of Squad officers were believed to be still missing 18 months after the PCA-supervised inquiry began, together with six files out of the 658 relating to arrests by Squad officers between 1st January 1986 and 14th August 1989, and an unknown number of other documents which should have been inside other files which have been recovered.

We are therefore concerned that the Serious Crime Squad's headquarters at Bradford Street police station were not properly secured to ensure that no documents could go missing before the investigating team from West Yorkshire police had been able to recover them. An inquiry carried out on behalf of the West Midlands Police Authority by Mr Roger Birch, Chief Constable of Sussex, concluded that this omission resulted from serious errors of judgement by senior police officers including the then Chief Constable Geoffrey Dear himself. Evidence in the possession of the inquiry team shows, however, that the mislaying of significant files (or of documents within them) was not uncommon so far as the Serious Crime Squad was concerned.

As a result of information received from protected informant Paul Jarvis (see above, p. 62), Mr Gerry Gall and others were tried for assault and unlawful possession of a firearm in early August 1989. Since being charged five months before, Mr Gall and his solicitor had endeavoured to obtain from the prosecution a file containing the victim's original statement in which he provided a description of his attacker. Both the police and the prosecuting authorities replied that they were unable to trace the file. However, during an adjournment for lunch on Tuesday, 8th August, the file suddenly re-appeared, in the words of Mr Gall's counsel, Mr Colman Treacy, 'like a rabbit out of a hat'. It had apparently been found in a box by Detective Sergeant James Milligan, who had earlier told the court that the file had been missing since 1988 without any indication as to who might have removed it. Yet when the relevant record book was produced, it showed that the file had been signed out to DS Michael Hornby. He said on oath that someone else must have booked the file out in his name as an administrative convenience, since he had not been responsible for its removal.

The file in question contained the original statement from the victim of the assault which described the appearance of his assailants. Neither Mr Gall nor any of his co-defendants bore any resemblance to this description, although they looked very like a description which the victim had given to Squad officers somewhat later. Each defendant was nevertheless convicted: judgment was given on the very day that the disbandment of the Squad was announced.

Meanwhile, two serving prisoners had made formal complaints about the way in which their own cases had been investigated. Mr Michael Brommell claimed that it was on the basis of a fabricated confession that he had been convicted in October 1987 of various shotgun offences for which he was sentenced to seven years' imprisonment. On 10th August 1989, Superintendent Derek Fancott of the force's own Complaints Department visited the archives at Warwick Crown Court in order to discover the identity of the officers involved. He found, however, that the allegedly contemporaneous notes of the relevant interview had been removed. Moreover, he was informed by the assistant that Detective Constables David Woodley and Roger Clifford had been to look at the very same file only the day before. They were suspended from duty on 14th August 1989, but were reinstated after an internal inquiry on 9th February 1990 concluded that there was no evidence that the pair had removed the file. The question as to why the notes were missing remains open.

On 11th August 1989, Superintendent Fancott attempted to obtain notes of an alleged interview with Gary Binham from the archives at Birmingham Crown Court. Binham had also been convicted, despite claiming that the evidence against him had been fabricated. Once again, the relevant documents were missing. He was also given leave to appeal despite the fact that the usual period allowed for making such an appeal had already elapsed.

Whereas many other forces have adopted a policy of keeping records of investigations for at least 10 years, the former West Midlands practice of shredding many original documents after just two years will inevitably hinder any attempts to discover whether a whole series of similar allegations can be substantiated.

Inconsistencies in recorded timings

Tom Davis, the English lecturer at the University of Birmingham who revealed the insertion of fabricated admissions in one of Paul Dandy's alleged statements, is regularly consulted as an expert in forensic analysis of handwriting in connection with criminal trials. He explained in a report to the inquiry team that the Home Office has conducted:

> a series of tests concerning speed of writing. They use experienced police officers, and have produced a set of rule-of-thumb criteria that, although they are not yet

published, they are prepared to use in court, to determine whether a given document could or could not have been written in a given time. They have found that a speed of 100-120 characters per minute (cpm) is readily attainable; 150 is difficult, but some people are capable of it; and the maximum that they found attainable was 172 cpm.

At our request, Mr Davis checked the timings of a random sample of 25 undisputed records of interviews of suspects carried out in the presence of a solicitor by police officers from different parts of the country. The interviews ranged in length from 12 minutes to 2 hours and 5 minutes. The fastest speed achieved by any note-taker was 145 cpm, which is approximately 30 words per minute (wpm). This interview had lasted 27 minutes. The mean average speed achieved was 108 cpm (about 23 wpm), whilst the median average was 106 cpm. Tom Davis therefore concluded that the Home Office figures are well supported by this project.

Calculations made by Mr John Bullivant while on remand for an alleged conspiracy to rob (of which he was subsequently acquitted) are therefore most revealing. He counted all the words alleged to have been uttered in interviews between Squad officers, his fellow accused and himself. He then divided the total by the number of minutes which the interviews were recorded as having lasted by Squad officers. The results are quite remarkable. Bullivant found that where the defence did not dispute the Squad record of an interview, the note-taker's speed varied between 11 and 21 words per minute, which is clearly within the range to be expected according to the figures obtained by both the Home Office and Mr Davis. However, the calculations for disputed statements showed that the writer generally managed to increase his speed to between 24.5 and 36 words per minute. In Bullivant's interview with DS Lloyd, DC Shaw apparently reached a writing speed of 128 words per minute! Significantly, this was the interview in which most of Bullivant's self-incriminating statements were supposed to have been made. Bullivant and his three co-accused were all acquitted by a jury (see Appendix B).

The same two Squad officers had been involved in the earlier case of Mr John O'Brien, who was tried in June 1987. During the course of their evidence, DS Lloyd and DC Shaw claimed that O'Brien had made a statement to them confessing to his part in a robbery. They said that it had taken just 14 minutes both to write down what O'Brien had allegedly said and to read it back to him. When Shaw, the note-taker, was required to repeat the task for the benefit of the court, it took him 21 minutes. The prosecution thereupon decided not to proceed with the case (see Appendix B).

In a further study for this inquiry, Tom Davis calculated the purported note-taking speed of 13 Serious Crime Squad officers in cases where the interviews recorded were carried out in the absence of any solicitor and the records have been disputed by the suspect interviewed. The speed achieved by 10 officers was below the maximum likely speed of 150 cpm. In the other three cases, however, the apparent speeds were 158 cpm, 163 cpm and 169 cpm respectively. Mr Davis concluded: 'It would seem that the speeds recorded [in these cases] are unlikely, but not impossible.'

A significant number of other inconsistencies appear in the timings recorded by Squad officers. Such inconsistencies may simply be the result of sloppy paperwork. This may, perhaps, explain a curious feature in the case of Mr Charles Campbell, who was arrested and convicted for armed robbery in March 1985 (i.e. pre-PACE). Although the times at which his interviews apparently began are noted, there appears to have been no record of when each interrogation was brought to an end.

Alternatively, inconsistencies in recorded timings after 1985 could be the product of a somewhat less than conscientious attitude towards complying with the requirements of PACE so that, for example, statements which were compiled by Squad officers *after* an interview may have been described by the officers as contemporaneous. The third, and most worrying, possibility is that these inconsistencies occurred because the statements in question were pure fabrication by Squad officers, so that the interviews which they purport to record may in fact never have taken place.

We have insufficient evidence on which to base a firm conclusion as to which of these scenarios is correct. One example which tends to support the third hypothesis, however, arises from the case of Hassan Khan, whose conviction for robbery was quashed by the Court of Appeal in February 1990 (see Chapter Four and Appendix B). The court noted that one of the major flaws in the prosecution case was that there were discrepancies between Squad officers' pocketbooks on the one hand and the custody sheet - compiled by a custody officer from outside the Squad - on the other, as to the times during which Khan was allegedly interviewed and made his confession.

Timings were also a matter of controversy in the case of the Birmingham Six, who were interviewed by the Serious Crime Squad in 1974. Home Office forensic scientist, Dr Frank Skuse, claimed to have administered his tests on the defendants somewhat later than was claimed by the defence, whose version of events was supported by a local chemist called in to supply Dr Skuse with the ether required. Dr Skuse had not kept contemporaneous notes of the tests, but his own recollection supported police records of the timings of the tests. This was important, since it tended to throw doubts on the claims of the defendants that they had been systematically beaten up by Squad officers much earlier on.

But it is not only the timings of interviews which complainants have alleged to be inaccurate. There is doubt, for example, about the precise time at which Mr Martin Foran was arrested in Hurst Street car park in Birmingham on 10th September 1984 for alleged robbery. The arresting officers claim that the time of his arrest was 3.05 pm, which was significant because an alleged accomplice claimed that he had arranged to meet Foran there at 3 pm.

However, Foran himself maintains that the arrest was effected at 2.05 pm, and that this was originally recorded on the custody sheet. Unfortunately, this document has been shredded in accordance with force practice, so that only a microfilm copy remains. This shows the time to be 3.05 pm, but this time appears next to another entry which has been crossed out. Forensic tests might have been able to prove something conclusive either way if the original document still existed, but in any case it is very doubtful that the time of 3.05pm is correct. For the same custody record also shows Martin Foran to have been in a cell at Bradford Street police station by 3.12 pm that same afternoon. Whilst both prosecution and defence agree that this entry is accurate, it is physically impossible for Mr Foran to have been arrested in Hurst Street, driven to Bradford Street, undergone normal custody procedures and been put in a cell within seven minutes, particularly at that time of day.

Furthermore, the interview during which Foran is alleged to have made some self-incriminating remarks is supposed to have concluded at 4.15 pm, and Foran is then said to have telephoned his solicitor at 4.50 pm. However, Mr J H Daniels, the legal executive sent by Foran's solicitor, is sure that he arrived at the police station - in response to the very same call - at 4.30 pm.

6

Squad Management and the Role of Senior Officers

The West Midlands Police Force is the second largest in the country after the Metropolitan Police. It was set up on 1st April 1974 as the result of the biggest merger of police forces ever undertaken in Britain. As Mr W H Werry, the District Auditor, noted in his *Review of the Management of West Midlands Police*, published in October 1985:

> The various demands which are... made on the force are obvious enough. Like the demands made on most police, however, they are singularly hard to reconcile. On one hand the public expects a higher level of protection against a wide spectrum of crime, from the most highly organised to apparently mindless. On the other hand law enforcement must, for social reasons, be more sensitive. The result is plain and is that policing has become immeasurably harder than it was even at the beginnings of the careers of many serving officers. (para. 5)

The District Auditor was, however, highly critical of the manner in which the force attempted to reconcile these objectives:

> [A] clear strategy is needed for coping with these pressures, but there is less agreement about what form it should take, and less still about how far any change should go. I feel myself that in the West Midlands it needs to go a long way. (para. 6)

Indeed, the West Midlands force's attitude towards management skills worried Mr Werry because senior officers played an unusually active role in the operational aspects of police work, rather than concentrating on providing effective supervision and leadership. Thus detective inspectors, for example, dealt with the paperwork involved in warning witnesses for court. Mr Werry also reported:

> I also was surprised at the number of officers who see and approve documents which are sent to third parties, and at the high level at which final approval is often given. All reports prepared by constables for example are seen by every grade up to superintendent. (para. 25.)

Of course, these officers would have had to report on Squad operations to those occupying more senior positions outside the Squad. Table 7 lists the names of those with responsibility for aspects of the Squad's management since its first full year of operation. In his Review of 1985, Mr Werry was extremely critical of the force's general approach to management. He said:

> an unduly high proportion of the supervision within the West Midlands force is paper supervision, and is no doubt a consequence of the volume of paper and of the centralisation of management.... Key managers within the force get no training in

management, and little discretion to exercise it. Some express acute frustration at this exclusion from management, but others are clearly habituated to it. (paras. 25, 22.)

Yet it was not until 1989 that Chief Constable Geoffrey Dear made management the subject of one of his force's five 'goals'. He explained in his Annual Report that his objective was:

To obtain 'value for money' by the most effective and efficient use of all resources in the pursuance of operational requirements.

Evidence of managerial inadequacies were reflected in a number of ways. One problem apparent from our study of the Annual Reports was the regular changes made to the manner of presentation of statistics. There is, for example, little breakdown of the reasons for Squad arrests in 1983 (see Table 3). This makes comparison from year to year unnecessarily difficult, but West Midlands Police were unable to provide us with an explanation as to the reasons for these changes in the presentation of statistical data.

Another problem, discussed earlier, was that successive ACCs (Crime) did not ensure a regular transfer of officers into and out of the Squad. It should be noted that one officer was allowed to remain in the Squad for a protracted period because of, in ACC Meffen's words, 'personal reasons'. Such longevity of service within one unit was a recipe for abuse, as Sir Robert Mark found in the Metropolitan Police. Indeed, the District Auditor's Review of 1989 commented that specialist squads were always a potential problem because :

their direct links to HQ and the fairly in-bred culture of CID must unbalance the operational command structure. (para. 83.)

The problem was exacerbated in relation to the Serious Crime Squad, for - although this has been officially denied - we believe that junior officers informally vetoed new recruits to the Squad. We are unaware of any officer from an ethnic minority having served in the Squad, and it is certainly the case that no woman ever did so. Such an abdication of managerial responsibility would explain the continual recruitment of similarly-minded detectives, often from the No. 4 Regional Crime Squad (see Chapter Two).

Yet another disturbing illustration of bad management practice surfaced during the trials of Messrs Brian Leslie Horobin and Kevin Wilcox. There was some controversy over the credibility of the evidence of certain Squad detectives, who were at the time the subjects of internal investigations arising out of the cases of Paul Dandy and Clifford Jones (see Appendix B). When the defendants appealed against their convictions for robbery, court officials sought clarification from the West Midlands Police about the nature of the allegations against the officers concerned. In a letter of 18th August 1988 purporting to come from a senior officer, but with an illegible signature, West Midlands Police replied to the Criminal Appeal Office in the following terms:

Consideration will be given via the [Police Complaints] Authority for disciplinary proceedings against the following officers of the Serious Crime Squad ...

The letter then listed the following officers, all of whom received punishment as a result of disciplinary proceedings: DC Shaw, DS Reynolds, DC Perkins, DS McManus and Det Supt Brown, together with one other Squad officer who was charged with having committed a disciplinary offence but was cleared. It continued:

The proposed disciplinary charges arise out of allegations now supported in part by handwriting evidence, that original contemporaneous notes were unreliable. *It is of importance to note that there were no incriminating admissions in the notes.* (Emphasis added)

In fact, ESDA tests in both the Dandy and Jones cases had shown that alleged admissions such as 'I planned it' were contained in statements which had been fabricated. Yet it was on the basis of this letter that the appeals of Horobin and Wilcox were turned down by the Court of Appeal in August 1988, for Lord Justice Stocker repeated: 'those records

TABLE 7: SENIOR OFFICERS WITH RESPONSIBILITIES FOR SQUAD MANAGEMENT 1975-89

Year	Chief Constable	Deputy Chief Constable	Assistant Chief Constable (Crime)	Head of CID (Operations)
1975	Mr P Knights	Mr C Gaskell	Mr H Robinson	Chief Supt R Scragg
1976	Mr P Knights	Mr M Buck	Mr H Robinson	Chief Supt T Meffen
1977	Mr P Knights	Mr M Buck	Mr H Robinson	Chief Supt T Meffen
1978	Mr P Knights	Mr M Buck	Mr F Jordan	Chief Supt T Meffen
1979	Mr P Knights	Mr M Buck	Mr D Gerty	Chief Supt T Meffen[1]
1980	Sir P Knights	Mr R Broome	Mr D Gerty	Chief Supt C Powell
1981	Sir P Knights	Mr R Broome	Mr D Gerty	Chief Supt C Powell
1982	Sir P Knights	Mr R Broome	Mr D Gerty[2]	Chief Supt C Powell
1983	Sir P Knights	Mr L Sharp	Mr T Meffen[1]	Chief Supt C Powell
1984	Sir P Knights[3]	Mr L Sharp	Mr T Meffen	Chief Supt T Moore
1985	Mr G Dear	Mr L Sharp	Mr T Meffen	Chief Supt T Moore
1986	Mr G Dear	Mr L Sharp	Mr T Meffen	Chief Supt J Byrne
1987	Mr G Dear	Mr L Sharp	Mr T Meffen	Chief Supt J Byrne
1988	Mr G Dear	Mr P Leopold	Mr T Meffen	Chief Supt J Byrne
1989	Mr G Dear	Mr P Leopold	Mr T Meffen	Chief Supt J Byrne[4]

1. In 1980 Chief Supt. Meffen was appointed Acting ACC (Crime) while Mr Gerty was engaged in an investigation into the Merseyside Police. Later in 1980 he became ACC (Support). He served in this post until appointed ACC (Crime) in 1983, in which year he also served as Acting Deputy Chief Constable until Mr Sharp took up this office.

2. Mr Gerty served as ACC (Personnel) during the years 1983-86 inclusive.

3. Now Lord Knights.

4. Moved to non-operational duties on 14th August 1989; restriction lifted on 28th June 1990.

do not include in any case alleged admissions having been made by any of the accused.'

The Court of Appeal had been completely misled. It is, however, unclear on whose authority the letter was drafted, and whether it was a negligent mistake or deliberately misleading. If the author was indeed a senior West Midlands officer, then this is clearly a matter of the utmost concern. If, on the other hand, the letter originated from someone of more junior rank - or from a junior civilian employee - then the concern must be as to how such a person was able to communicate with the Court of Appeal over such an important matter without proper supervision. But whichever possibility is true, the management systems of West Midlands Police were clearly defective.

Moreover, before the original trial of Mr John Edwards, who was convicted in 1988 of robbery, his solicitor wrote to the Crown Prosecution Service (CPS) asking if any of the officers involved were under investigation. He was informed that DC Shaw was being investigated, but Shaw had only interviewed one of Edwards's co-defendants. The CPS failed to mention that DCI John Brown - then Head of the Serious Crime Squad and the officer in charge of Edwards's case - was facing disciplinary charges. Mr Edwards's conviction has now been quashed (see Appendix B).

In a third case, counsel for Mr Tony Wellington, who was convicted of armed robbery in 1988, was incorrectly informed that no officers in the case were under investigation. In fact, DC Woodley, the officer who took notes of Mr Wellington's interrogation, was being investigated. The defence alleged that pages five, six and seven of the eight-page interview record were fabricated. These were the only pages to contain admissions to the robbery in question. Wellington consistently denied any involvement, and his conviction was quashed by the Court of Appeal in March 1991.

It is not known whether the inaccuracies in the replies to the legal representatives of Edwards and Wellington were due to an oversight by the CPS or by someone in the West Midlands police force whom the CPS contacted for information.

Geoffrey Dear became Chief Constable for the West Midlands force in 1985, having previously served in the Metropolitan Police. He is now Inspector of Constabulary for the Midlands. Other than the failure to ensure the securing of Bradford Street police station on the disbandment of the Squad, we have found no evidence of any direct mismanagement or culpability on Mr Dear's part. The severe criticism levelled at the bureaucracy of the whole West Midlands police force, by both ourselves and the District Auditor, should not be taken as implying criticism of Mr Dear. The first - and more critical - of the District Auditor's reports was, after all, published in the very year that Mr Dear became Chief Constable and should therefore be seen more as criticism of the administration of his predecessor, Sir Philip (now Lord) Knights.

During his term of office Mr Dear attempted to instigate some improvements in efficiency, and these are noted in the District Auditor's report of 1989. However, any organisation which requires 17 different types of document in the purchase of its cars is clearly rather set in its ways and will be slow to respond to the changes demanded of it. This was particularly so in the case of the Serious Crime Squad which (as we explained in Chapter Two) resisted change in the face of several initiatives from the Chief Constable to improve Squad practice and efficiency.

Furthermore, in response to increasing speculation that the Serious Crime Squad was engaged in systematic malpractice, Mr Dear enquired of the Police Complaints Authority whether it had any evidence to substantiate this claim. When the Authority replied in the negative, Mr Dear decided to carry out his own review of the Squad's activities, which culminated in an announcement in June 1989 that it was to be re-organised. When it became clear in the summer of 1989 that more drastic action might be necessary, Mr Dear responded swiftly by disbanding the Squad in the August of that year.

However, to our knowledge, Mr Dear did not address a West Midlands practice which, as far as we are aware, is mirrored by no other force in the country. This was the policy of destroying all documents relating to criminal investigations after just two years. Exceptions were made when thought necessary, but the majority of such documents were simply shredded, having first been copied onto microfilm. In the course of our research we have found many such copies to be almost worthless, for they frequently omit vital details and in some cases are barely legible. Most important of all, however, is that it is quite pointless to carry out forensic or ESDA examinations on documents other than originals. We therefore find this practice quite extraordinary, particularly since police officers are obliged to keep their own notebooks for a minimum of seven years; it is also the policy of the Lord Chancellor's Department to maintain all trial records for a minimum of seven years. Solicitors to whom we have spoken have adopted similar guidelines.

There is one other issue which causes us some difficulty. It concerns Mr Dear's announcements that 53 present and former members of the Serious Crime Squad were to be moved to non-operational duties - a statement repeated in his introduction to the 1989 Annual Report which was presented to the West Midlands Police Authority (p.xiii). Yet his successor, Mr Ronald Hadfield, maintained at a press conference on 28th June 1990 that only 36 officers had been affected in this way (News Release, 28th June 1990, p. 6). Since we have been denied access by the West Midlands Police to the relevant records, we are unable to reconcile these statements; nor can the Police Complaints Authority. We consider this to be a very unsatisfactory state of affairs, not least because it is impossible to ascertain both whether all the officers whom Mr Dear proposed should be moved were in fact transferred, and whether former Squad officers have had any restriction on operational duties lifted.

7

Summary of Findings and Conclusion

Findings

1. The inquiry investigated 67 Serious Crime Squad cases between 1979 and 1989 involving around 170 suspects and defendants. *(Page 19)*

2. We are aware of 23 trials of Serious Crime Squad cases involving the unsuccessful prosecution of 41 defendants, where either the charges were dropped, the judge directed acquittal, the jury found the defendants to be innocent or where the conviction was quashed on appeal. *(Appendix B, page 87)*

3. The forbear of the Serious Crime Squad was formed in February 1952 as part of the City of Birmingham police. *(Page 20)*

4. The Squad's performance - measured by the number of arrests made by Squad officers - fell significantly during the 1980s. *(Table 2, page 22 and pages 23-6)*

5. Much of the Squad's work was not related to very 'serious' cases at all. *(Table 3, page 23 and page 24)*

6. Many officers served in the Squad for very long periods. *(Table 6, page 29 and pages 27-8)*

7. The Squad developed its own ethos, and its machismo culture deterred female officers from applying to serve within it. *(Page 28)*

8. The Squad was highly resistant to change and/or reorganisation. *(Page 28)*

9. The Squad operated in crews of three, with one detective sergeant and two constables. *(Pages 30 and 42)*

10. Squad officers saw themselves as an élite body within the West Midlands force. *(Page 30)*

11. Much of the Squad's effort in investigating crime was channelled into attempts to obtain confessions from suspects. *(Page 38)*

12. Interviewing techniques and guidelines outlined in the West Midlands Police Interview Development Unit's course manual appear dangerously simplistic. *(Page 41)*

13. Regular partnerships of Squad officers are over-represented in the number of Squad prosecutions in the 1980s which failed because of defects in the prosecution evidence. *(Pages 42-3 and Appendix B, page 87)*

14. Squad officers followed no particular pattern in selecting a police station in which to interview suspects. *(Page 47)*

15. Relations between Squad officers and those on divisional duties were rather strained. *(Page 47)*

16. A large proportion of Squad arrests were effected in the early hours of the morning. *(Page 47)*

17. Access to legal representation was delayed in every case (except one) where the presence of a solicitor was requested by the suspect. *(Page 48)*

18   Our investigation bears out research carried out for the Royal Commission on Criminal Procedure (Irving and Hildendorf, 1981), which found that very few interviewees possessed the 'iron will' to remain silent under questioning unless in the presence of a solicitor. *(Page 48)*

19. In none of the cases that we have investigated have suspects made any incriminating statements while in the presence of their own solicitors. *(Page 48)*

20. The Squad carried out remarkably few interrogations after the defendants' legal representatives had arrived at the police station. *(Page 84)*

21. Allegations of physical abuse of suspects in the earlier years of our study were frequent, but from about 1986 onwards the number of such complaints declined significantly, to be replaced by a significantly larger number of complaints of threats of physical violence. *(Page 52 and Appendix B, page 87)*

22. Section 30 of PACE (which requires that where a person is arrested for an offence he should be taken to a police station as soon as practicable thereafter) was incorrectly applied by Squad officers. *(Page 55)*

23. In every one of the Serious Crime Squad cases which have been submitted to this inquiry, it has been alleged that officers from the Squad fabricated incriminating admissions. *(Page 56)*

24. In every case submitted to us which went to trial on the basis of evidence obtained by the Serious Crime Squad, an alleged confession formed the cornerstone of the prosecution; in many cases an uncorroborated and disputed confession was the sum total of the Crown's evidence. *(Page 56)*

25. Some of the confessions allegedly made by suspects in the custody of Squad officers lack significant details. *(Page 57)*

26. The phraseology of different suspects' interview records appears strikingly similar in a significant number of cases examined by the inquiry. *(Pages 57-8)*

27. According to the purported interview records submitted to the inquiry, the recorded speech of interviewer and interviewee often appears to be in the same vernacular even though the suspect does not originate from the West Midlands. *(Page 58)*

28. The Police Complaints Authority has refused to let complainants see a copy of their own statements made to West Yorkshire officers investigating on the PCA's behalf despite the enactment of section 98(1)(a) of PACE. *(Page 58)*

29. Throughout the 1980s the Serious Crime Squad relied heavily on information provided by protected police informants or 'supergrasses'. *(Pages 60-61)*

30. The offices of the Serious Crime Squad at Bradford Street police station were not properly and expeditiously secured when the Squad was disbanded. *(Page 63)*

31. The mislaying of significant files and/or documents was not uncommon as far as the Squad was concerned. *(Page 63)*

32. Home Office criteria - regarding handwriting speeds which are used as rule-of-thumb guides to determine whether or not a given document could have been written in a given time - were well supported by a random sample of undisputed statements obtained by this inquiry. *(Page 65)*

33. The handwriting speeds necessary to take down 10 statements from Squad suspects but alleged to be fabrications were found to be readily attainable according to the Home Office figures. *(Page 65)*

34. The handwriting speeds necessary to take down a further three disputed statements were found to be unlikely but not impossible. *(Page 65)*

35. There are a number of instances in which the times of events recorded by Squad officers appear to be inconsistent with each other. *(Page 66)*

36. The ability of senior officers in West Midlands Police to manage their responsibilities effectively was severely hampered by too much unnecessary paperwork and inadequate or insufficient training. *(Pages 67-8)*

37. All original documents relating to criminal investigations by West Midlands Police were destroyed after two years unless considered sufficiently important to warrant safekeeping, a practice out of step, as far as we are aware, with other forces elsewhere in the country. *(Page 71)*

38.   We are unable to reconcile the announcement in August 1989 by the then Chief Constable, Geoffrey Dear, of the transfer of 53 present and former members of the Serious Crime Squad to non-operational duties with the later statement made by his successor, Mr Ronald Hadfield, that only 36 officers had been so transferred. *(Page 71)*

Conclusion

We have presented evidence of malpractice in the West Midlands Serious Crime Squad based on a snapshot of cases. With evidence drawn from only 67 Squad cases, there is nothing to suggest that all officers who served in the Squad are implicated. However, there is obviously genuine cause for concern as to whether there have been other cases where malpractice of the sort identified in this report has occurred but has never come to light.

8

Recommendations

Confession evidence

It is clear from this project's research that the main problem with the working practices of the Serious Crime Squad concerned suspects' alleged confessions and their status as admissible evidence in court. In Scotland such admissions are not admissible unless corroborated by some other evidence (see Chapter Four). Many people have suggested that if the law of England and Wales were to adopt the same position, many of the worst abuses and errors would be eliminated.

The distinguished former Law Lord, Lord Scarman, has been one of the most notable advocates of this amendment to the law. He has said:

> No conviction should be allowed on the basis of exclusive and uncorroborated confession evidence. If the only evidence is a confession obtained in a police station or by a policeman in other circumstances, there should be no conviction. (*Panorama*, 5th March 1990)

We respectfully agree.

Recommendation I

> *No confession should be admitted in evidence unless it is supported by other non-confession evidence.*

However, we are not convinced that this argument goes far enough. Indeed, we are concerned lest a disputed confession and otherwise weak evidence elsewhere in the prosecution case are held to be mutually corroborative. There is also the possibility that, having obtained a confession (whether by fair means or foul), the police may sometimes find it hard to resist fabricating the required corroborative evidence. The cases of Ronnie Bolden and Robert Burston *et al* (see Chapter Five and Appendix B) are examples of just such abuse.

We welcome the moves towards the tape-recording and video-recording of evidence but we do not believe that the tape-recording of interviews will prevent the occurrence of all wrongdoing by detectives in future. It is possible to exert psychological pressure in ways that are not revealed by a recording. Moreover, such stress is exceedingly difficult for a dispassionate third party - like a judge or jury - to detect from merely listening to, or viewing, the recording. This problem can be exacerbated when only relatively short excerpts from a recording of an interview, lasting perhaps two or three hours, are replayed in court. Of course, non-verbal threats by police officers such as pretending to punch the suspect, or threatening him with a hypodermic syringe (such as George Glen Lewis alleges) could not possibly be recorded on audio tape.

A further problem is that no one has ever suggested that any of these technological aids should be used when interrogations are conducted outside police stations. Yet the alleged 'car seat confessions' (see Chapter Four) show how important it is that steps are also taken to regulate, control or abolish such interviews. We therefore believe that additional safeguards are also required.

Recommendation 2

Informal interviews, chats, conversations, discussions, talks or other forms of communication between suspect and police officer - whether at the scene of the crime or in police vehicles or on the way to the cells or elsewhere - should not be admitted in evidence.

Recommendation 3

No confession should be admitted in evidence unless it has been tape-recorded or recorded on video tape.

Recommendation 4

All confessions obtained in breach of PACE or the Codes of Practice or otherwise unfairly obtained must be automatically excluded. Where at present the trial judge has a discretion as to whether to admit or exclude this evidence, this discretion should be replaced with an obligation to exclude the evidence. This requires amendments to section 76 of PACE. As a minimum measure, a rule could be developed which would involve the exclusion of evidence to a degree commensurate with the seriousness of both the breach of PACE and the crime alleged.

Recommendation 4 would enforce proper behaviour on the part of the police, since evidence obtained by means of underhand practice or downright criminal behaviour would not be admissible as evidence in court. But probably the best safeguard against accusations of fabricated confessions (whether proven or not) is the presence of a solicitor during a suspect's interview.

Recommendation 5

No confessions should be allowed into evidence except where the statement in question has been freely given in the presence of the defendant's solicitor (or, where the suspect declines to appoint a legal representative, the duty solicitor) unless voluntarily confirmed by the defendant in court.

This would have the effect of 'balancing up' the interview, so reducing the likelihood that stress would produce a false confession. It would also ensure the presence of an independent witness to each interview, although there would not necessarily be any such witness to what takes place prior to such interviews. Such a safeguard would also be valuable in those instances where a defendant is alleged to have uttered a remark such as 'You now know how it happened', which apparently confirms the authenticity of an alleged confession by a co-defendant. If the presence of a solicitor were made a mandatory requirement for all interrogations, it would be possible to use one person's alleged confession as evidence against a co-defendant only if both the original confession and the subsequent admission by the co-accused had both been freely and fully given in the presence of a solicitor. This measure would, of course, require an injection of greater resources into the duty solicitor scheme in order to ensure that solicitors were always available to attend police interviews.

Recommendation 6

> *We are also implacably opposed to the abolition of a suspect's right to remain silent under police questioning in England and Wales, consideration of which has been deferred but not abandoned following its abolition in Northern Ireland in 1988.*

Irving and Hildendorf (1981) demonstrated clearly that suspects in police custody are easily pressurised. There may well be, therefore, very good reasons for remaining silent when interrogated. Moreover, if this right is reinforced by the requirement of a solicitor's presence for all interrogations, it will be rather easier actually to exercise this right than hitherto.

Recommendation 7

> *We urge strongly that the present rule requiring the corroboration of supergrass evidence be retained.*

It has recently been suggested that the evidence of supergrasses should no longer require corroboration before a defendant can be convicted on such evidence. This is in line with a general trend away from requiring corroboration. The cases examined by the inquiry team suggest, however, that this may be a dangerous step to take, since supergrasses have such clear material incentives to give their evidence in the manner most favourable to the prosecution.

Complaints

Although we have made a number of criticisms of the practices of the Police Complaints Authority and those working under its supervision, it does at least have the responsibility of supervising allegations of misconduct by individual police officers. It is a matter of some concern to us, however, that although the activities of individual officers are often simply the result of the implementation of policies which have been inadequately thought out beforehand, there appears to be no body corresponding to the PCA charged with reviewing general policing strategy and its implementation.

It will be recalled, for example, that Clare Short MP was told in January 1989 by the then Minister of State at the Home Office that the Inspectorate of Constabulary was not the appropriate body to carry out such a task. And although the District Auditor may make recommendations to improve economic efficiency, there is no one to review matters of operational policy. This seems to us to be an anomalous omission. Public utilities, for instance, have their policies under constant review by an official agency acting as a consumer watchdog. Similarly, the activities of government departments are constantly scrutinised by select committees.

Recommendation 8

We strongly recommend that either the Police Complaints Authority or, preferably, the Inspectorate of Constabulary, should have its remit extended so as to include responsibility for carrying out periodic reviews of operational police policy.

Recommendation 9

Staff of both the PCA and Inspectorate should receive specific training in criminal law and criminology, and should be recruited from both the police and outside organisations so as to include lay persons.

Recommendation 10

We recommend that a standard presentation of statistics should be adopted by all police forces in order to facilitate meaningful interpretation.

For whatever reason, the presentation of statistics in the West Midlands police force seems to have undergone such regular revision that it is often extremely difficult to make meaningful comparisons of the performance either of the force as a whole or of particular sections within it such as the Serious Crime Squad.

Recommendation 11

Until such standardisation has been accepted, however, we recommend that each police authority equip its Chief Constable with guidelines as to the manner in which statistics should be reported in the Annual Reports presented to it.

Recommendation 12

No documents should be shredded by police forces or reduced to microfilm or microfiche until a minimum period of seven years has elapsed since its last use for any legal purpose, in accordance with the practice of both solicitors and Crown Courts.

Recommendation 13

Breaches of PACE or of COP should no longer be treated purely as disciplinary offences. Instead they should in future be treated as grounds for a civil action in the law of tort, so as to enable those suspects who have suffered as a result to claim compensation for such loss.

Recommendation 14

Investigations into complaints against police officers should begin as soon as possible after they are received, and should not be deferred until after the completion of any related criminal or civil proceedings.

Recommendation 15

All official complainants making statements to police officers acting under the supervision of the Police Complaints Authority should be entitled to receive and keep a copy of any written record of such statements in order to check their authenticity and accuracy.

Recommendation 16

There should be a duty on those informing a complainant of the outcome of his/her complaint to give full reasons for the complaints being upheld or rejected. The present standard letter, which contains only the final decision, would therefore be insufficient.

Special squads

There can be no doubt that the formation of special units such as the Serious Crime Squad involves the creation of an élite group, which is expected to be able to achieve results that ordinary officers on divisional duty have been unable to obtain. In such circumstances there is always a risk that a squad whose arrest and detection record does not justify its own existence may resort to improper methods in order to survive. Specific measures must therefore be taken to guard against this eventuality. Although it appears unlikely that a successor to the Serious Crime Squad will be formed in the West Midlands force in the foreseeable future, it is important that other similar squads - both in the West Midlands and elsewhere - ensure that every possible measure is taken to prevent the occurrence of similar malpractice.

Recommendation 17

It is most important that when specialist squads are created, they are given a clearly-defined role within CID.

This is vital in order to ensure that they do not simply re-investigate crimes which have already been the subject of divisional inquiries. Such a duplication of work by the Serious Crime Squad was extremely inefficient, and was also the cause of unconstructive friction between Squad and divisional detectives.

Recommendation 18

The precise role and relevance of specialist squads must also be kept constantly under review. Police forces must not be reluctant to disband squads which are felt either to be inefficient or simply to duplicate work better performed elsewhere. If the reason for creating the squad in the first instance disappears, that is prima facie good reason for the expiry of the squad itself.

We are unhappy that the terms of reference of the Serious Crime Squad seemed regularly to have changed because the relevance of earlier tasks had significantly diminished (see Chapter Two). A more appropriate course of action might have been to close down the Squad altogether. Despite the existence of the Serious Crime Squad, for example, a specialist Robbery Squad was nonetheless created in 1977 to deal with the Thursday Gang: once the gang had been broken up in 1981, the Robbery Squad was disbanded.

Once a new squad has been established, we are in complete agreement with the District Auditor (see Chapter Six) that senior officers should be both allowed and encouraged to manage it without the burden of unnecessary paperwork which can be done by junior officers.

Recommendation 19

We believe it to be imperative for senior officers to retain full control over the recruitment of new squad personnel. Particular attention should be paid to the recruitment of female officers and officers from ethnic minorities.

Recommendation 20

Any formal attempt by junior officers to discourage the application and/or recruitment of particular officers should be firmly resisted. Any such behaviour on an informal level (see Chapter Two) should be strongly discouraged to the extent that anyone indulging in such conduct should be transferred from the squad in question.

We do not, however, believe that merely transferring officers from divisional work and placing them in a special unit is in itself sufficient to achieve the goals sought.

Recommendation 21

For such a group to be effective, its members must undergo specialist training which is geared both to the squad's particular tasks and to its officers' special requirements. Senior officers, too, should receive special training in the necessary management skills.

Recommendation 22

There should be a formal appraisal every year of each officer's conduct, competence and suitability for service in the squad in question.

We believe that this is now the norm in police forces nationwide.

Recommendation 23

No officer should be allowed to serve continuously in a specialist squad for more than two years unless there are good reasons for waiving this restriction. We believe that such good reasons exist in the case of officers serving in child liaison and fraud squads, for example, where it often takes two years to learn the special skills required. In these cases a five-year limitation would seem more appropriate.

Recommendation 24

Any officers seeking to return to a specialist squad should only be permitted to do so after a minimum of two years has elapsed since the completion of the previous period of service.

Police discipline

We commented in Chapter Six on the poor management of the Serious Crime Squad by senior officers. At the same time we pointed out that, even if they had been significantly more vigilant, their ability effectively to discipline the officers under their command would have been severely restricted by the requirements of the Police Discipline Regulations (summarised in Chapter Three). As Laurence Lustgarten has written, 'The police are a uniquely favoured class of wrongdoer.' (1986, p. 153).

Recommendation 25

We would strongly urge that the Police Discipline Regulations be revised at the earliest opportunity.

We are not alone in holding this view. The suggestion that there is a need to review the police discipline code has received some support from the present Metropolitan Police Commissioner, Sir Peter Imbert. In an interview on BBC1's *Panorama* programme, broadcast on 5th March 1990, Sir Peter said:

Under the disciplinary code the burden of proof is such that one has to have absolute proof, to prove the case beyond reasonable doubt, before that person can leave the service. Some officers hide behind the system and that is inevitable. If there are one or two hiding behind the system, we have got to see how the system can be changed.

Recommendation 26

We recommend that the present requirement that all disciplinary charges be proved beyond reasonable doubt be abolished. Instead, the standard of proof should be the same as for civilian employees, which is that an employer must be satisfied on the balance of probabilities that the complaint has been sustained.

The adoption of such a standard of proof in police disciplinary hearings would mean that the requirements of proof in court would no longer be much the same as that before a disciplinary tribunal. There would no longer be any reason, therefore, to maintain the rule against so-called 'double jeopardy', whereby a police officer cannot be disciplined for substantially the same offence for which s/he has previously been charged - whether convicted or acquitted - in a criminal court.

Recommendation 27

We recommend the abolition of the 'double jeopardy' rule.

Again, this would bring employment within the police service into line with that in civilian life. Of course, in order to compensate serving police officers for their loss of protection from arbitrary management, it would be necessary to provide them with some new form of employment protection.

Recommendation 28

We recommend that police officers be given the full employment protection rights of civilian employees: they should have the right both to a written statement of the reasons for their dismissal and the right not to be unfairly dismissed.

APPENDIX A: INVESTIGATIONS OF POLICE BY POLICE 1989-90

Force Investigated	Investigating Force	Subject of Allegation
Cambridgeshire	Norfolk	Harassment
Cleveland	Northumbria	Failure to find body of Julie Hoggbehind bathroom panel until 10weeks after reported missing
Essex	Sussex	Bribery and corruption in No. 5 Regional Crime Squad
Essex	Kent	Unknown[1]
Essex	Suffolk	Unknown[1]
Gloucestershire	Hertfordshire	Unlawful arrest
Greater Manchester	West Yorkshire	Suppression of evidence; consorting with criminals and conspiracy
Humberside	West Yorkshire	Senior officer kerb-crawling
Humberside	Unknown[1]	Death in custody
Kent	Hampshire	Falsification of crime statistics[2]
Kent	Essex	Unknown[1]
Merseyside	West Yorkshire	Fabrication of evidence; planting of drugs; assault and intimidation by 30 officers
Metropolitan	Hampshire	Corrupt investigation of Catford murder

Force Investigated	Investigating Force	Subject of Allegation
Metropolitan	Northamptonshire	Brutality at Wapping
Metropolitan	Hertfordshire	Leak to BBC of report by Northamptonshire police in Wapping case
Metropolitan	Thames Valley	Second Inquiry into 3 of the most serious of Wapping cases which led to civil actions
Metropolitan	Hampshire	Shooting of armed robbers
Metropolitan	Hertfordshire	Planting of drugs and assault[3]
Northumbria	Cumbria	Corruption
Northumbria	Cumbria	Perjury and intent to pervert the course of justice
Nottinghamshire	Leicestershire	Fabrication of confession
Royal Ulster	Cambridgeshire	Leaking information to paramilitaries[4]
South Wales	Devon & Cornwall	Murder investigation
South Yorkshire	Greater Manchester	Falsification of evidence and assault by officers in No. 3 Regional Crime Squad
South Yorkshire	Nottinghamshire	Fabrication of evidence and conspiracy
South Yorkshire	West Midlands	Hillsborough
Surrey	Avon & Somerset[4]	Guildford Four
Thames Valley	Surrey	Unknown[1]
Thames Valley	Hertfordshire	Unknown[1]

Force Investigated	Investigating Force	Subject of Allegation
Thames Valley	Bedfordshire	Unknown[1]
Thames Valley	Unknown[1]	Unknown[1]
West Midlands	West Yorkshire	Serious Crime Squad
West Midlands	Sussex	Failure to secure Serious Crime Squad headquarters upon announcement of Squad's dissolution
West Midlands	Devon & Cornwall	Birmingham Six
West Yorkshire	Greater Manchester[4]	Arson investigation
West Yorkshire	North Yorkshire	Improper internal inquiry into investigation of child's death
West Yorkshire	South Yorkshire	Murder investigation

1. Neither the Police Complaints Authority nor the police forces involved were prepared to release the relevant information.
2. A superintendent retired on medical grounds without charges against him being heard. As a result of disciplinary hearings a sergeant was dismissed from the force, five officers were fined between £50 and £250, and 25 officers were admonished or advised.
3. The Police Complaints Authority declined to publish its report, although the 18 complainants were told of the outcome of their cases. There are to be no criminal or disciplinary proceedings against any Notting Hill officers. One complainant, Rupert Taylor, was awarded damages of £100,000 against the Metropolitan Police (including £70,000 exemplary damages to mark the jury's disapproval of police conduct) for false imprisonment and malicious prosecution. The sum awarded is believed to be a record for damages against the police.
4. Unsupervised by the Police Complaints Authority.

Of the 43 police forces of England and Wales:

i) at least 17 have been investigated by another force in the past two years;
ii) at least 22 have carried out such investigations (whether supervised by the PCA or not); and
iii) at least 10 have both carried out and been the subject of such investigations.

APPENDIX B: UNSUCCESSFUL PROSECUTIONS OF SERIOUS CRIME SQUAD CASES KNOWN TO THE INQUIRY TEAM 1981-91

Case	Defendant	Detectives[1]	Alleged defect in case	Outcome	Date
1.	David Moss Rashan Khela Brian Ward John Rowley Malcolm Firkins James Redmond John Braniff	Unknown[2]	Confessions obtained improperly	Charges dropped	27.3.81
2.	Carla Nota Antonio		Fabricated confession	Acquitted by jury	July 1982
3.	George Twitchell		Inconsistent timings Defendant subjected to duress	Acquitted by jury	July 1982
4.	Derek Gordon[3]		Fabricated confession	Charges dropped	1983
5.	Malcolm Herring	DI Matthews	Fabricated confession	Acquitted by jury	Nov. 1985
6.	William Barrett Calvin Walters Donald Patterson		Fabricated confessions; Planted evidence	Acquitted by jury	9.10.86 10.10.86
7.	Clifford Jones John O'Brien Chris Turner Harry Elwell	DS Hornby[4] DC McLelland[4] DC Shaw[5] DS Lloyd[5] DS Reynolds[7] DC Perkins[8]	Fabricated confessions; Inconsistent timings; Prosecution tainted by Jones case	Judge directed acquittal[6] Charges dropped	25.6.87
8.	John Bullivant Hubert Forbes Leo Morgan Wesley Stewart	DS Ford DC Quin DS Reynolds DC Perkins DS McManus DC Adams	Fabricated confessions; Planted evidence; Inconsistent timings;	Acquitted by jury	11.7.87

Case	Defendant	Detectives[1]	Alleged defect in case	Outcome	Date
		DS Lloyd DC Shaw DS Swinnerton DC Rawlings DS Hornby DC McLelland	Flawed identification evidence; Missing document		
9.	Paul Dandy	DS McManus[9] DC Shaw[9] Det Supt Brown[9]	Fabricated confession	Charges dropped	Nov. 87
10.	Norman Manning Derek Manning		Prosecution tainted by Dandy case; Planted forensic evidence	Charges dropped	Feb. 88
11.	Vincent Palmer		Prosecution tainted by Dandy case	Charges dropped	17.3.88
12.	Jahved Akhtar Tracy Evans		Improperly organised identity parades	Judge directed acquittal	27.4.88
13.	Eileen McCabe		Confession given under duress; Improper denial of access to solicitor	Judge directed acquittal	1988
14.	Leroy Francis; Ramsingh Nowjadicksingh	DC Shaw	DC Shaw discredited as reliable witness; Missing surveillance evidence	Acquitted by jury	1988
15.	Paul Fitzsimmons	DS McManus DC Adams	DS McManus discredited as reliable witness; Confession given under duress; One exhibit lost	Judge directed acquittal[10]	Oct. 88

Case	Defendant	Detectives[1]	Alleged defect in case	Outcome	Date
16.	Robert Burston Alexander Davies Ernest Callaghan Anthony Waldron		Original notes of interviews missing; Fabricated forensic evidence	Judge directed acquittal	7.12.88
17.	Paul Harris	DS Hornby DC McLelland	Fabricated confession; Improper denial of access to solicitor	Judge directed acquittal	25.4.89
18.	Ronnie Bolden	DS McManus DC Adams DS Hornby DC McLelland	Fabricated confession; Fabricated attempted bribe by defendant's solicitors; Fabricated forensic evidence	Acquitted by jury[11]	22.6.89
19.	Keith Parchment		Inconsistent timings; Fabricated confession	Conviction quashed on appeal	17.7.89
20.	Harry Allan	DC Woodley	Undue pressure on witness	Charges dropped	29.1.90
21.	Hassan Khan	DCI Goodchild DS Howkins DS Swinnerton DC Rawlings DC Leary	Fabricated confession; Inconsistent timings	Conviction quashed on appeal	23.2.90
22.	John Edwards	DC Shaw DS Bowen DC Woodley DC Quin DS Owen	Fabricated confession; Inconsistent timings; Incomplete information supplied to defence lawyers	Conviction quashed on appeal	16.1.91
23.	Tony Wellington	DC Woodley	Fabricated confession	Conviction quashed on appeal	25.3.91

1. We have only included here detectives already referred to in the text.
2. The Lord Chancellor's office has declined to release full details, but it is known that two unidentified officers were suspended, but that the Director of Public Prosecutions ruled that there was insufficient evidence to prosecute them.

3.   Awarded £20,000 damages for false imprisonment. Two unidentified officers were not disciplined, but were given advice about standards of documentation.
4.   Subject of an internal investigation for alleged falsehood by falsifying notes, but not charged with any criminal or disciplinary offence.
5.   Charged but cleared of disciplinary offence of falsehood for alleged falsification of notes.
6.   Judge Christopher Stuart-White wrote to the Chief Constable about the conduct of the police in this case, calling for an inquiry into the 'wholly unsatisfactory state of the evidence'.
7.   Found guilty of disciplinary offence of falsehood for making false and untruthful records. Demoted to rank of uniformed police constable.
8.   Found guilty of disciplinary offence of falsehood for allegedly making false and untruthful records. Fined 13 days' pay (approx. £500), which is the maximum permissible fine under police regulations.
9.   Reprimanded for the disciplinary offence of neglect of duty for losing a page of interview notes.
10. Judge Malcolm Potter wrote to the Chief Constable asking him to clear up DS McManus's credibility.
11. After a re-trial was ordered by the judge because of the allegation that the defendant's solicitors had attempted to bribe a witness.

APPENDIX C: SENIOR OFFICERS TRANSFERRED TO NON-OPERATIONAL DUTIES ON 14TH AUGUST 1989

Name & Previous Post	*New Post*
Det Chief Supt Jim Byrne[1] *Head of West Midlands CID*	*Research & Development Unit*
Det Chief Supt Michael Holder[2]	*Community Support Services*
Det Supt Stan Beechey[2] *Deputy Head of West Midlands CID* *Former Head of Serious Crime Squad*	*Studying technical aspects* *of Hillsborough*
Det Supt John Brown[3] *Deputy Head of No. 4 Regional Crime Squad*	*Policy Review Department*
Det Supt Roger Corbett *Head of CID, 'B' Division*	*Personnel Department*
Det Supt Brian Davies *Queen's Road, Aston CID* *Penultimate Head of Serious Crime Squad*	*Routine Administration at* *Headquarters*
Det Supt Bob Morris[2] *Head of West Midlands Drugs Squad*	*Studying Football Crowd* *Control after Hillsborough*
Det Chief Insp Ray Bennett[2] *Head of Serious Crime Squad*	*Crime Prevention*
Det Chief Insp Bob Goodchild *Head of Chelmsley Wood CID*	*In charge of road safety* *and talks in schools*
Det Chief Insp Henry Martyn Thomas[2] *City Centre CID Office*	*Administrative Duties*
Det Insp William Gwilt[2]	
Det Insp Peter Higgins[1]	
Det Insp James Kelly	

1. Returned to operational duties on 28th June 1990.
2. Returned to operational duties on 30th November 1990.
3. Disciplined for disposing of the original record of an interview with Paul Dandy.

APPENDIX D: POLICE DISCIPLINARY OFFENCES: EXTRACTS FROM THE POLICE DISCIPLINE CODE

1. **Discreditable conduct,** which offence is committed where a member of a police force acts in adisorderly manner prejudicial to discipline or reasonably likely to bring discredit on the reputation of the force or of the police service.

3. **Disobedience to orders,** which offence is committed where a member of a police force, without good and sufficient cause -
    (a) disobeys or neglects to carry out any lawful order, written or otherwise; or
    (b) fails to comply with any requirement of a code of practice for the time being in force under section 60 or 66 of [PACE]; or
    (c) contravenes any provisions of the Police Regulations containing restrictions on the private lives of members of police forces, or requiring him to notify the chief officer of police that he, or a relation included in his family, has a business interest within the meaning of those Regulations.

4. **Neglect of duty,** which offence is committed where a member of a police force, without good and sufficient cause -
    (a) neglects or omits to attend to or carry out with due promptitude and diligence anything which it is his duty as a member of a police force to attend to or carry out; or
    (b) fails to work his beat in accordance with orders, or leaves the place of duty to which he has been ordered, or having left his place of duty for an authorised purpose fails to return thereto without undue delay; or
    (c) is absent without leave from, or is late for, any duty; or
    (d) fails properly to account for, or to make a prompt and true return of, any money or property received by him in the course of his duty.

5. **Falsehood or prevarication,** which offence is committed where a member of a police force -
    (a) knowingly or through neglect makes any false, misleading or inaccurate oral or written statement or entry in any record or document made, kept or required for police purposes; or
    (b) either wilfully and without proper authority or through lack of due care destroys or mutilates any record or document made, kept or required for police purposes; or
    (c) without good and sufficient cause alters or erases or adds to any entry in such a record or document; or
    (d) has knowingly or through neglect made any false, misleading or inaccurate statement in connection with his appointment to the police force.

7. **Corrupt or improper practice,** which offence is committed where a member of a police force -
    (a) in his capacity as a member of the force and without the consent of the chief officer of police or the police authority, directly or indirectly solicits or accepts any gratuity, present or subscription; or
    (b) places himself under a pecuniary obligation to any person in such a manner as

might affect his properly carrying out his duties as a member of the force; or

(c) improperly uses, or attempt to use, his position as a member of the force for his private advantage; or

(d) in his capacity as a member of the force and without the consent of the chief officer of police, writes, signs or gives a testimonial of character or other recommendation with the object of obtaining employment for any person or of supporting an application for the grant of a license of any kind.

8. **Abuse of authority,** which offence is committed where a member of a police force treats any person with whom he may be brought into contact in the execution of his duty in an oppressive manner and, without prejudice to the foregoing, in particular where he -

(a) without good and sufficient cause conducts a search, or requires a person to submit to any test or procedure, or makes an arrest; or

(b) uses any unnecessary violence towards any prisoner or any other person with whom he may be brought into contact in the execution of his duty, or improperly threatens any such person with violence; or

(c) is abusive or uncivil to any member of the public.

9. **Racially discriminatory behaviour,** which offence is committed (without prejudice to the commission of any other offence) where a member of a police force -

(a) while on duty, on the grounds of another person's colour, race, nationality or ethnic or national origins, acts towards that other person in any such way as is mentioned in paragraph 8 (abuse of authority); or

(b) in any other way, on any of those grounds, treats improperly a person with whom he may be brought into contact while on duty.

11. **Improper dress or untidiness,** which offence is committed where without good and sufficient cause a member of a police force while on duty, or while off duty but wearing uniform in a public place, is improperly dressed or is untidy in his appearance.

13. **Drunkenness,** which offence is committed where a member of a police force tenders himself unfit through drink for duties which he is or will be required to perform or which he may reasonably foresee having to perform.

14. **Drinking on duty or soliciting drink,** which offence is committed where a member of a police force, while on duty -

(a) without proper authority, drinks, or receives from any other person, any intoxicating liquor; or

(b) demands, or endeavours to persuade any other person to give him or to purchase or obtain for him any intoxicating liquor.

16. **Criminal conduct,** which offence is committed where a member of a police force has been found guilty by a court of law of a criminal offence.

17. **Being an accessory to a disciplinary offence,** which offence is committed where a member of a police force incites, connives at or is knowingly an accessory to any offence against discipline.

REFERENCES

Baldwin J and McConville M, 'Police Interrogation and the Right to see a Solicitor', *Criminal Law Review*, 1979, p. 145.

Baldwin J and McConville M, *Courts, Prosecution and Conviction*, (Oxford: Oxford University Press, 1981).

Bottomley K et al, 'Safeguarding the Rights of Suspects in Police Custody', *Policing and Society*, 1990, p.115.

Brown D, *Police Complaints Procedure - A Survey of Complainants' Views*, (London: HMSO, 1988).

Gudjonsson I and Mackeith J, 'Retracted Confessions', *Medical Science and the Law*, 1988, vol. 28, p. 187.

Irving B, *Police Interrogation: A Case Study of Current Practice*, (London: HMSO, 1990).

Irving B and Hildendorf L, *Police Interrogation - The Psychological Approach*, (London: HMSO, 1981).

Irving B and McKenzie I, 'Interrogating in a Legal Framework' in Morgan and Smith, *Coming to Terms with Policing*, (London: Routledge, 1989).

Lustgarten L, *The Governance of Police*, (London: Sweet and Maxwell, 1986).

Maguire M and Corbett C, 'Patterns and Profiles of Complaints against the Police' in Morgan and Smith, *Coming to Terms with Policing*, (London: Routledge, 1989).

Morgan R and Smith D, *Coming to Terms with Policing*, (London: Routledge, 1989).

Sanders A, 'Rights, Remedies, and the Police and Criminal Evidence Act', *Criminal Law Review*, 1988, p. 802.

Sanders A et al, *Advice and Assistance at Police Stations*, (London: Lord Chancellor's Department, 1989).

Sanders A and Bridges L, 'Access to Legal Advice and Police Malpractice', *Criminal Law Review*, 1990, p. 494.

Selwyn N, *Selwyn's Law of Employment*, 6th ed., (London: Butterworths, 1988).

Softley P, *Police Interrogation - An Observational Study*, (London: HMSO, 1980).

Zander M, 'Access to a Solicitor in the Police Station', *Criminal Law Review*, 1972, p. 342.